RESOLVING CLASSROOM CONFLICT

by Craig Pearson
with the editors of LEARNING magazine

LEARNING Handbooks
530 University Avenue
Palo Alto, California 94301

FOREWORD

Cooperation, communication and awareness can grow in your classroom. This book offers suggestions, insights and experiences which may help you to build a responsible, equitable classroom.

The purpose of this and other LEARNING Handbooks is to help make teaching and learning more effective, interesting and exciting. Craig Pearson is an education writer, developer of teaching materials and president of Education Ventures, Inc., Middletown, Connecticut.

The author wishes to acknowledge his indebtedness for the cooperation and insights of many skilled teachers, particularly Marge Altman, Dave Audette, Jack Brogan, Bud Church, Clare Clark, George Cocores, Bob Connelly, Joel Davis, Peter Dublin, Lee Dyer, Melanie Gaimei, Barbara Kiesel, Karen Knapp, Frank LaBella, Ron McMullen, Irving Oullette, Larry Sage, Steve Solomon and Cynthia and Mario Tucciarone.

EDITOR: Carol B. Whiteley
DESIGNER: David Hale
PHOTOGRAPHY: Ken Sherman Pages 4, 16, 20, 25, 30, 41, 48, 53, 62, 71, 80, 84, 88; ASI, Inc. Pages 10, 36, 66, 74; Curtis A. Reif Pages 45, 56; Boris of Boston Page 74.
COVER ART: Lars Speyer and Cummings Walker

EXECUTIVE EDITOR: Morton Malkofsky
DESIGN DIRECTOR: Robert G. Bryant

Library of Congress Number: 74-16805
International Standard Book Number: 0-915092-01-8

Book Code 003 • Third Printing February 1977

CONTENTS

CHAPTER 1

WHAT'S THE PROBLEM?

ISSUES gain genuine stature when they make the funny papers. The question of conflict, for example, was dignified by its appearance in an installment of "Blondie." Cora Dithers, battle-ax wife of Dagwood's boss, shows to Blondie a thick book called *How to Avoid Conflict in Marriage*.

"Does it work?" asks Blondie.

"It sure does," says Mrs. Dithers. "Whenever Julius gets out of line, I hit him with it."

If the reader confidently foresees similar utility in this work, *Resolving Classroom Conflict*, it is probably now appropriate for you to stop reading the book and start wielding it. If, on the other hand, the reader feels that classroom conflict is challenging, enlightening, counterproductive, distracting, debilitating, honest, potentially constructive, invigorating—we encourage you to read on.

Just what is classroom conflict? Talks with dozens of classroom teachers suggest two general and contrasting definitions:

1. Classroom conflict=disruption of classroom order.
2. Classroom conflict is a disagreement of needs which often leads to disruption (active or passive) of classroom effectiveness.

The range of difference between the two can be seen in five teachers' working definitions:

"Conflict happens when one or two people disturb all the rest. No matter how many options you give them, they show no motivation, do no work, don't keep quiet. You wouldn't mind it if they just sat there. In fact, my classes are pretty noisy, and I can stand the general roar when good work is happening. But then you get the noises that are different from all the rest. You get the war whoops and bird calls that mean some kids

6

arc not working and are trying to rattle all the rest who are working. They're always testing the limits. Maybe the hard rules and heavy authority of the past made it easier on the child as well as the teacher. . . ."

"Conflict is any friction—between children, between child and teacher, teacher and teacher, parents and teacher, parents and children—which has an effect on the learning environment."

"It seems to me that conflict is of two kinds. One is the personality conflict between child and teacher—the student just doesn't like the teacher. The other is conflict among children. It seems to me that our traditional grouping procedures bring all sorts of neighborhood squabbles and playground disagreements into the classroom, where they are acted out in aggressive behavior. Finally, the teacher has to act as referee."

"I try to think not about classroom conflict but about my own inner conflict. I blame myself, not the first graders, when I lack an answer or when my answers cancel out. But when the situation's very sticky, I sometimes find myself falling back on the old power solution. I have to say, 'Cut it out. I'm making the rules!' But I'd rather not."

"Classroom conflict? It's just any problem that exists in the classroom which disturbs the teacher and the children. No, I don't think it's just a matter of classroom disorder. After all, whose order is being disrupted? Mostly the teacher's. But class size is a problem that keeps you from getting at other problems. . . .They've just added child number 26 to my kindergarten. . . ."

A KID'S EYE VIEW

And what about the kids? The definition of classroom conflict becomes more exacting when expressed by students:

"The teacher keeps mispronouncing my name. It's hard to pronounce. It's Deirdre—Deer-dreh. And he keeps calling me Deedree or Day-id-dree or something else. I keep correcting him, but he keeps on doing it. The worst part is that he keeps acting as though he's right and I'm wrong. . . ."—Seventh grader

"Everybody was drawing pictures of ocean liners. We all put in the portholes, and then we all put in the smokestacks. But I put in the flag too soon. The teacher came over and she saw my paper—she took it and ripped it up in front of the whole class. She told everybody else I didn't follow instructions. I was ashamed. And mad, too."—Third grader

"Everything is very tight, and staying in line. I try to stay out of trouble. But I got in trouble. There's this teacher named Miss Campbell. She's very picky. She walks on her toes and she wants everybody else to walk on their toes, too. She's a good teacher, I guess, but I hate her guts. I was out in the playground and I saw her leaning out the window and all of a sudden I yelled, 'Campbell Pork and Beans!' I don't know why. I had to go to the principal's office. I was scared. He told me to behave better. But he was kind of smiling. That was strange. . . ." —Sixth grader

"The trouble is my mouth. I'm always in the corner because I'm always talking. Then I listen. The teacher's always teaching, but the kids aren't getting it."—Fifth grader

"There's a lot of boredom. We do pages of math problems and turn them in and then we have to sit quietly and do easy kinds of seatwork while the teacher goes over the math with the slower kids, one or two at a time. I'm good at math. One day, I was listening to a kid having trouble with the answer to problem number 20, and I raised my hand and said I remembered the answer. I can actually remember all the answers. But the

teacher gave me a funny look—she has a jaw that sticks way out—and she said, 'Your paper is here. How could you possibly remember that?' But I told her again that I did, and she said, 'All right, what is the answer?' So I told her. But she looked angry just the same."—Fifth grader

"*I'm a good boy. But it's dull. The same thing all the time, and once in a while a movie. . . .*"—Fourth grader

THE WORST THING ABOUT SCHOOL

Most of the above testimony suggests open or hidden conflict—but it also involves the liberal exercise of editorial license. The students just quoted are actually practicing classroom teachers, role-playing their own childhood recollections of "the worst thing about school." Accumulated as evidence, teachers' memories may add up to a story of conflict no less imposing than the comments of education's most severe contemporary critics:

"*. . . . It is not possible to spend any prolonged period visiting public school classrooms without being appalled by the mutilation visible everywhere—mutilation of spontaneity, of joy in learning, of pleasure in creating, of sense of self. The public schools . . . are the kind of institution one cannot really dislike until one gets to know them well. Because adults take the schools so much for granted, they fail to appreciate what grim, joyless places most American schools are, how oppressive and petty are the rules by which they are governed, how intellectually sterile and esthetically barren the atmosphere, what an appalling lack of civility obtains on the part of teachers and principals, what contempt they unconsciously display for children as children.*"—Charles Silberman, *Crisis in the Classroom: The Remaking of American Education* (New York: Random House, 1970), p. 10.

"*. . . . The schools assume built-in motivation, but when it does not occur, they attempt to motivate children with methods analogous to using a gun. Although guns have never worked, the schools, struggling to solve their problems, resort to using bigger and bigger guns—more restrictions and rules, more threats and punishments. . . .*"—William Glasser, M.D., *Schools Without Failure* (New York: Harper & Row, 1969), pp. 18-19.

"*. . . . We have learned that most of these [educational] pr*

The teacher's always teaching,
but the kids aren't getting it.

*fessional people are remarkably similar to parents in their atti-
tudes toward kids and in their methods of dealing with them.
They, too, usually fail to listen to children; they, too, talk to
children in ways that put them down and damage their self-
esteem; they, too, rely heavily on authority and power to ma-
nipulate and control children's behavior; . . . they, too, hassle
and harangue and preach and shame children in attempts to
shape their values and beliefs and mold them into their own
image."* —Dr. Thomas Gordon, Parent Effectiveness Training:
The No-Lose Program for Raising Responsible Children
(New York: Wyden, 1970), p. 298.

*"In the face of many uncertainties, the teacher may feel a
desperate need for exercising rigid control within the classroom to insure that at least the outward appearance of constructive effort is maintained. When students seem orderly
and attentive, it is easier for the teacher to feel assured that he
is teaching successfully. Deviations from accepted behavior
patterns must be sternly suppressed, because they destroy
this sense of confidence. . . . Some teachers appear to live in
dread of insurrection, obsessively concerned with preserving
order in the classroom at all costs. Coercive measures pre-
dominate; reproaches fill the air. Inordinate amounts of time
are spent enforcing minor regulations. . . . The student re-
gards the teacher not as one who guides and assists but as one
who threatens and invokes penalties. A gulf widens between
students and teacher. The classroom becomes an arena of op-
posing forces rather than a laboratory for learning."* —Robert
H. Snow, "Anxieties and Discontents in Teaching," Phi Delta
Kappan, 1963, 44, pp. 318-321, as reprinted in Henry Clay
Lindgren, Readings in Educational Psychology (New York:
John Wiley & Sons, 1968), p. 455.

These educators offer megaton criticisms. Yet their thoughts are
formed by the innumerable atoms of conflict experience that practicing teachers recognize, from past and present. Though the testimony about it is not ample, substantial numbers of today's teachers
may have entered education in order to change it. Some have surely
started out with the goal of mending the framework which permitted
their own childhood misfortunes. "I loved learning in spite of the
boredom and routine of school," says one teacher, "and I kept going
back to it." Yet many such teachers have found themselves seemingly doomed (if the critics are correct) to repeat and reinforce his-

11

tory, and—for a host of expedient reasons—to treat children as they were once treated.

VISIBLE AND INVISIBLE CONFLICT

The earlier-quoted critics' key word is "power," which they define as an imposed discipline which is oppressive, anti-intellectual and inhumane. A move from the classroom level to the policy/administrative level in the ordinary school system will also find the terms of power expressed openly and heavily. The administrator, confronted with suggestions for modest relaxations of the learning or conduct code, responds with his "reductio ad absurdum"—stretching the proposal to its most ridiculous extreme: "But you *can't* let kids do *anything* they want to!" A school board member calls discipline a "finger in the dike"—flood control or flood, absolute command or absolute anarchy.

The author once discussed with a principal the proposition that students might have school rights parallel to adult civil rights. The principal responded almost violently. "You can't run a school *that* way," he asserted, banging the table with untypical fervor. The same gentleman hypothesized at another time that the teaching of discipline—teaching children how to accept control—was the *main* function of the school, and that subject matter and curriculum concerns were indeed secondary to that prime goal.

Classroom-level power questions are philosophically pale by comparison. The classroom teacher, handling literally hundreds of intellectual and emotional transactions every hour, simply has no time to wrap experiences up in weighty generalizations. Yet the effects of the power equation in school conflict—rules incite challenges incite more rules incite more challenges—are evident in many simple guises. One teacher, for example, empathized with the librarian in his middle school:

"Ann won't let the kids whisper, and they really dislike her because of it. She doesn't deserve it. She's a good librarian. But she knows the kids are always going to test the limits. If she lets them whisper, someone's going to murmur. And if she lets them murmur, someone's going to talk out loud. And if she lets them talk, someone's going to yell. So she doesn't let them even whisper."

That situation, and its thousands of classroom counterparts, may indeed be tolerable on the grounds that there is an appearance of order and no *visible* sign of conflict. The class or the school may fulfill requirements with a controlled level of student sullenness, passivity and withdrawn behavior. Some students may even seem nervously eager to comply with rules and directions (though these same children, as Dr. Thomas Gordon points out, may become "the adults who fill the offices of psychologists and psychiatrists"[1].

There is little possibility that the teacher who honestly finds such conditions adequate will be interested in resolving questions of conflict.

More intensely committed teachers may recognize the withdrawn or "tuned-out" child as the most desperate of conflict problems. One teacher vividly describes them as "my failures: the indifferent or lost or too-soft or too-hard kid who sat in the back of the room like an impressionistic painting or a piece of slowly spoiling meat, and shut me out. . . ."[2]

CONFLICT RESOLUTION IS A TWO-WAY CHANNEL

In conflict situations, some teachers may be attracted to techniques of behavior modification. Behavior modification systems simply do not fit into the theme of this book, since their elaborate conditioning-reward approaches (as distinguished from control-punishment methods) remain a matter of manipulating the child from an adult command post. Critics rightfully argue that this is a way of *training* rather than *educating* the child. Conflict resolution, by contrast, is most aptly defined as a two-way channel of analysis and negotiation. It might be characterized in the words of the old businessman who says, "No deal is any good unless it's good for both sides."

The most compelling arguments for conflict resolution in the classroom have been made over the past 15 years by humanistic psychologists, operating on the basic premises that:
1. No person can be taught what he/she is unwilling to learn.
2. No person can be compelled to be responsible and self-directing.

It would be incongruous, however, to suppose that a teacher should at once submit to the most authoritative views on non-authoritarianism—the rules for dispensing with rules. The contrariness of that notion is nevertheless more common than it ought to be, as when teachers are *commanded* to be more democratic, or *told* to undertake, without inquiry of their own, more inquiry skills training for their students. This is the stuff of administrative fiat, and it suggests relationships that look like one of those traditional college board questions:

Student is to *teacher* as *teacher* is to: (a) superintendent; (b) school

[1]Gordon, op.cit., p. 183.

[2]Diana L. George, "Why I Quit," Changing Education (Summer 1974), p. 15.

board; (c) public opinión; (d) culture.

In a rule-bound tradition, *all* those answers are "right," and it is assumed that the teacher will toe the mark, professionally. What else is the teacher to do when faced with a sudden mandate to "Grow," "State Objectives Behaviorally," "Innovate," "Career-ize," "Individualize" or "Be Humane"? In fact, teachers can (and do) use some of the very tactics which work so well for children in contending with the overweening power of the system. Usually, it's a form of going limp, or demonstrating an automaton-like willingness to accept all commands, slowly, painfully and a bit cynically. But how is the teacher to build commitment to the "new whatever-it-is" on the basis of a two-week, in-service workshop recipe? This is one more way of creating conflicts rather than resolving them.

IT TAKES COMMITMENT

Most teachers operate under constant heavy pressure that pushes them all over a continuum like this one:

Absolute	Conflict	Outright
Command	Resolution	Permissiveness

Some may occasionally achieve the Summerhillian end of the rainbow where children live in perfect freedom as perfect learning humans. Some are stuck at the left of the continuum as perfect unblinking tyrants, totally oblivious to the needs of children, to knowledge or to anything but the rules. Most are involved in a process of seeking classroom equity in the way that Abraham Lincoln said general equality had to be sought: ". . . constantly looked to, constantly labored for, and even though never perfectly attained, constantly approximated, and thereby constantly spreading and deepening its influence and augmenting the happiness and value of life to all people. . . ."[3]

One teacher dedicated to openness grants that there are occasions for emergency power: "You can't just let things fall apart." But she tries to make this reasoning the exception rather than the rule.

Another teacher remembers an incident that might defy classification:

"This eighth grade boy, bigger than me, shouted out something really filthy. What made it worse was his acting as though he didn't

---

[3]Speech at Springfield, Ill., June 26, 1857, as quoted in *A Treasury of Lincoln Quotations* by Fred Kerner, New York: Doubleday, 1965, p.55.

know what it meant. I felt as though I'd really sock him in the jaw if I could have gotten across the room fast enough. Instead I found myself yelling back at him, 'How would you like a good swift kick in the ass?' Unprofessional as hell. But the kid was friendly and polite, all the rest of the year."

So the teacher exerted power, threatening forceful punishment.

But no, it wasn't a true threat; crude as the response was, it was a genuine, personal statement about how the teacher felt. A student can respect that kind of feeling, where he can't respect impersonal power.

What follows is not a *Better Homes and Gardens* feature on "How to Build a Better Classroom in Ten Easy Steps for Under $29.50." The subsequent chapters offer classroom teachers' comments on conflict situations categorized as child vs. child, child vs. teacher, child vs. system, child/teacher vs. system. Some may seem ambiguous, some are sparklingly commonsensical. And while none are prescriptions, four practices can be abstracted from them:
1. Ask students what their trouble is, and be open about what is troubling you.
2. Listen, really listen, to what they have to say.
3. Keep in touch with problems instead of shipping them out in form letters or delegations to the principal's office.
4. Find out how far you can limit rules instead of expanding them.

These are not four dandy ways that will instantly change your role as a teacher and improve your life. But they can be implemented as you try to evolve a personal way of dealing with conflict and build a responsible, equitable classroom. The society of many classrooms keeps building itself out of responsible individual commitments, and that is what most of the rest of this book is about.

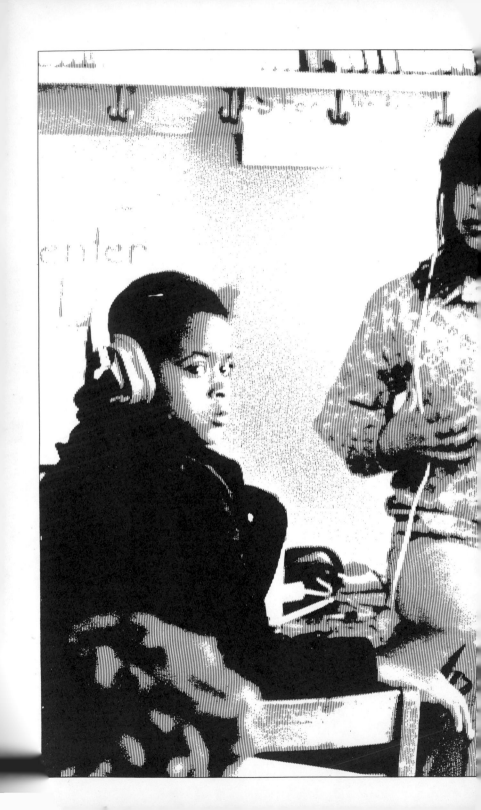

CHAPTER 2

CHILD VS. CHILD VS. CHILD VS. CHILD.....

THE broadest potential for classroom conflict lies in the basic natures of children. Kids come to school *already* arrogant, timid, consumed by fear, compulsively neat, haughty, aggressive, withdrawn, overadventurous, stealthy, even precociously sexy or pedantic. Some, as well, may be physically malformed or mentally malnourished in ways that make them noticeably different from the rest (though not different enough to qualify them for an institution).

None of this is the teacher's fault. At nursery school, kindergarten or first grade level, the teacher hasn't had the faintest influence over the formative environments—mainly paternal and familial, but also economic and social—from which the children emerge. Prior schooling may soon be added to this list of environmental factors, but, at the beginning of the year, the upper grade teacher may have had only nominal influence on that.

Thus there is no serious reason to consider the teacher responsible for the way children are—responsible for the three of 30 potential "problems" who walk in the classroom door on the first day of school.

But detachment can go just that far. As soon as they meet, the pre-formed nature of the child confronts the particular philosophy of the teacher. And the teacher may be convinced, in biblically simple terms, that human nature is pernicious (needing constant restraint) or that it is innocent and perfectible (needing only to be nourished).

One source offers a beginning teacher's observations after her

18

very first day in full charge of a second grade classroom:

"Actually, I felt that everything that happened was very important for me as well as for the children. Getting them set in their routines, starting work, getting them used to writing in their notebooks, giving orders to them to do certain things was very important to me. I really felt very good giving them these orders and telling them what to do. Now I had the power position for once!

"The best thing that happened to me on the first day was being such a tyrant and not showing that I was a softie right away. I figured while I was sitting there that the children were probably hating me but I wasn't taking it to heart because I wanted to get them straight right away on what I expected of them and not let them take advantage of me.

"At three o'clock I said, 'Good afternoon, class,' and waited for their reply. As we walked out of the door everyone ran over and started to kiss me, which I let them do the first day because I couldn't help it. They all surrounded me. This sort of made me feel very good, knowing that I really didn't let them get away with anything and getting the satisfaction that these children would cooperate. . . . Actually, nothing really bad happened the first day. . . .The children did whatever I said and no one talked back to me. . . ."[1]

---

[1]Estelle Fuchs, *Teachers Talk: Views from Inside City Schools* (Garden City, N.Y.: Doubleday Anchor Original, 1969), pp. 9–10.

Perhaps most teachers begin with self-generated expectations that children will naturally be "bad" or naturally be "good." The young teacher quoted above believed that the children would instinctively try to "get away with something." She was relieved to find them "co-operative" instead but she was hardly reassured that she could drop her guard without something "really bad" happening. Why did she not assume, on the basis of a day's evidence, that these children were naturally attentive, industrious, self-directed and loving?

Most of us, however, have had our own formative environments which color our assessments of day-to-day evidence. Deep cultural or religious training, or philosophical reflection, have put us on one side or the other in the ancient debate over people being inherently good, or inherently wanting direction away from evil

The natures of children intrude upon almost every classroom as boredom, terror, mischief, insolence, rebellion or violence.

inclinations. Where one stands in this everlasting argument may be a fundamental question in teaching style. Do you see yourself embellishing the natural goodness of your students' lives? Do you see yourself regulating and reforming student natures which are basically flawed? Or have you found a way to distinguish between good-natured and bad-natured, assuming each to be exclusive and unchangeable? This sort of self-questioning is vital, since it may show that "teacher-nature" as well as "child-nature" may well be the grounds for classroom conflict.

CLASSROOM BEHAVIOR REFLECTS TEACHER TOLERANCE

Many of the teachers whose comments make up much of this book observe that the very definition of "bad" behavior can be quite

flexible; that rules are often based on highly predictable types of behavior—running, talking, squirming, jostling, hitting, giggling—*purely* to generate conflict, thence a need for punishment and a demonstration of control is made obvious. This sort of morality play may be known as "showing the kids who's boss." By contrast, other classrooms may tolerate and absorb some extraordinary actions—one student's physical tantrum, another's shouting of four-letter words or a hair-pulling fight between two girls—without general breakdown or even loss of general decorum. The tolerable range of behavior in either case is set by the teacher's gauge of the contagiousness of conflict behavior.

At times, either view can work wonders in surmounting the causes of conflict. There are classrooms where students function like a precision drill team, apparently so overjoyed by hours of well-regulated living that their individual frustrations and eccentricities are subdued or forgotten. They primly learn what they are told, and there are no visible signs of hostility, sullenness or withdrawal. (There is hardly time for that in the tight routine.)

Punishment is a well-known part of the classroom code, but it has fallen into disuse. ("The kids *believe* I'd hit them if they pushed me too far," one teacher observed. "I never would. But they think I would. That's enough. I don't get any trouble.")

There are also classrooms where the children's engagement with intellectual content is so freewheeling and so vividly compelling that individual differences are literally put out of mind. The very flow of the lesson dominates the life of the classroom. The very thought of disciplinary rules and punishment is vestigial; they simply don't matter.

It might be argued that the effectiveness of the first class makes the substance of learning insignificant, while the second may lack some essential tension of social or emotional interaction. Both types of classes, at any rate, are highly improbable in the schools as we know them. The natures of children and their individual problems are so insistently powerful that they will intrude upon almost every classroom in some form of dramatized boredom, visible terror, mischief, insolence, rebellion or violence.

HANDLE IT YOURSELF—OR FIND AN EXPERT?

When conflict happens and the cause (as is usual) is perceived to spring from the child's aberrant needs, the teacher has two options, both ostensibly sensitive and responsible. The first might be called *Freudian*, to the extent that it seeks to piece together a picture of all the deep sources of the child's behavior. It demands that the problem be moved out of the classroom and into the view of experts, who may include the principal, the counselor, the parent, the social worker, the physician and the psychologist.

The second option, approximating the *gestalt* approach—or "here-and-now" psychology—is more accessible to the individual teacher simply because it does not tolerate all the deep-lying explanations of why a person's behavior is the way it is. It merely asks what the behavior really *is*, and how it can be changed.

The recourse to experts, as many teachers know, may be far less responsible than it seems. There are simply too few experts who have too few hours, in most situations, to do what they are asked to do. Often they can provide only the appearance of conflict resolution, as one urban school psychologist testifies in describing the case of a 9-year-old third grader:

"After three or four letters and threats of suspension, Mama comes to school—with two smaller children: the two year old blissfully unperturbed and the four year old terrified (he's already gotten the word from Mama that schools are bad places). Before the teacher can begin to recite her long list of grievances against the child, Mama loudly bemoans the fact that her boy will not listen to her and that she cannot do a thing with him; he fights with his brother and takes money from her purse and cannot read at all—and what is the school going to do about it? Teacher is understanding and has listened sympathetically, but now informs Mama that the child (who is standing right there) talks in class, walks out of the room without a pass, does not do his homework, and stole a pencil from the little girl next to him. Mama gets up and whacks the kid across the head. . . .

"The problem continues. Several more fruitless punitive measures are taken; but, since teachers are much harder to come by than pupils, the boy must be disposed of. . . . The principal turns to the school psychologist. He asks me to arrange for a Medical Suspense. . . . As a green school psychologist, I do not react favorably to this request. From years of clinical experience, I know that the child is not seriously disturbed. And, in any case, I do not see the sense in just sending him home without any plan for helping him to adjust to the madness around him. I suggest setting up a special class for problem children like him. But there are not enough rooms or teachers or both, and the principal does not believe it is fair to the majority of children to deprive them of facilities because of a deviant few. Deadlock!

"I return to the teacher. . . . I explain to her that the child she referred to me cannot be placed in a special class or school, as he is neither retarded nor psychotic; that his behavior disorder is so

23

grounded in pervasive family pathology and social chaos that even if I had the time to work with him on a regular basis (impossible with four schools to cover), he is not likely to change appreciably. . . .

"We commiserate. . . . Finally, I ask if she can manage him for half a day. She admits the boy's behavior generally does not become uncontrollable until after lunch and agrees to schedule him mornings only, on a trial basis. I consult with the principal, who, relieved by any solution, agrees; and with the mother, who figures half a day out of her hair is better than nothing. I propose the new plan to the little boy. He says he does not care either way; and he really means it."[2]

THE TEACHER CAN BE AS EFFECTIVE AS THE SPECIALIZED THERAPIST

In cases like the preceding one, the teacher's professional conscience must be concerned with reasonable doubts on two levels. One is the grounds for referral: By the standards of the teacher and/or the school, the child is seriously disturbed (or disturbing); by the psychologist's norms of mental health, the child is not seriously disturbed. The second question involves the effectiveness of referral: Should the teacher start the process at all if she knows that workable resources can't be marshalled in the child's behalf?

Often, the exporting of problems from the classroom is clearly perceived by the teacher as a matter of personal survival dominating personal competence and professional ethics. ("When you send 'em to the principal," said one interviewee, "you're admitting defeat. When the only possibility left is sending the child out of the classroom, you've just run out of skill."

Psychologist Ron McMullen (former Associate Director of Wesleyan University's Upward Bound Program and a lecturer in education at the African-American Institute) suggests, in amiable conversation, that the dilemma needn't exist if specialization can be taken less seriously:

"The importance of (us) psychologists is overblown. Basically, we're in the rent-a-friend business. Kids—or teachers, for that matter—need a friend who will talk with them about their problems and be truthfully critical about what's wrong without being threatening or punitive. Psychologists provide that service. We're trusted because we're outsiders.

---

[2]Stephen B. Goldman, "Notes of a Green School Psychologist," The Urban Review, vol. 4, no. 2 (October 1969), p. 19.

Often, the exporting of problems from the classroom is clearly perceived by the teacher as a matter of personal survival.

"Since there are simply not enough psychologists to go around, anyway, we'd just as well think about people closer to the scene learning how to be friends. Take a situation more distressed than the schools: In mental hospitals, someone finally realized that the psychiatric aides spent far, far more time with patients than the psychiatrists—the experts. So they reasoned that the aides should be trained in therapeutic techniques, in order to be more supportive of the total effort, or at least not to subvert it. The results, when aides were given some of the doctors' skills, were pretty astonishing.

"Now teachers, if they are not in fact part of the problem, are a lot better situated than psychiatric aides to be part of the solution. By intelligence, calling, and training, they are ideally qualified to be the detached friend who can moderate the kid's problems with his environment. Given a small repertoire of therapeutic techniques, the teacher can be as effective or more effective than the specialized therapist or counselor."

BE DETERMINED—OR MIND YOUR OWN BUSINESS?

A teacher's sense of competence in handling conflict situations may seem to be almost stubbornly insensitive. Yet one respondent's belief in rigorous self-sufficiency proved to be right in one of the most sensitive conflict situations imaginable:

"I have a lot of faith in myself. My sixth graders are with me about six hours a day. If I'm preoccupied with the *causes* of their life problems, investigation is all I'm going to do. I don't have time for that. Personally, I want to provide a positive experience for the student all the time he is in school. I believe the teacher can be an alternative force in the student's life."

"One boy comes in worn out and ragged every Monday morning. I know why he's tense and tired. His parents have been bombed out and brawling all weekend long. And you and I and a dozen social workers aren't going to change the facts of that kid's home life. Should we bring the parents in? Nonsense. That way, we're simply laying one more negative aspect on that student's school experience. In fact, I'm not too comfortable with some learning specialists, or with remedial anything—remedial programs *need* failures to support them.

"No, I don't think I'm evading knowledge about who my students are. For example, there was the case—an extreme case—of a girl whose problem behavior included a magnified hatred of male teachers. I mean *hate*. She had a whole pattern of really poisonous looks, and an exaggerated keeping of distance with male staff members—this was noticeably missing from her relationships with

26

female teachers. I had my own dark suspicions about why, but I wasn't about to delegate them to specialists without evidence, or to her family—where they'd probably have gotten me shot—or to take what would seem to be the easy way out by transferring her to a female teacher. I decided instead that I was going to demonstrate to her that men are not all that bad by treating her with every bit of dignity and courtesy I could muster.

"She seemed to settle down as weeks went by, but the year was practically over before she demonstrated any real trust in me. When she did, it was shattering. She came to my desk one day when I was alone and, bursting into tears, told me that she had been sexually molested by a male relative. I was then able to help her talk to other authorities. I think I was right in handling the situation this way. But you can never be sure. . . ."

As this teacher knows, there is bound to be self-doubt about self-sufficiency (or playing God?) in the confines of a classroom. Could he have subjected the child to further danger by keeping his suspicions to himself? Is "Mind Your Own Business" a fair guideline for teachers in dealing with children's behavior when accredited expertise—however limited—is available outside the classroom?

LET THEM KNOW YOU CARE

A third grade teacher comments on a situation in which she tried, with some apparent success, to liberate one boy from an extensive therapeutic process:

"I like to work with children myself, keeping them in the classroom. Maybe I'm oversensitive. But it seems rewarding to me. Digging into their personal lives may be necessary, but only to the extent that it applies to something in school. Basically, I guess, I don't want to know much about where they came from, but only who they are. I surely don't like to have them go through lots of social work and psychological attention, which seems to me only to label them as more different and troubled than ever.

"I couldn't follow my own rules with Jimmy. He was under psychiatric care when he came to my classroom several months into the school year. He'd moved in with foster parents in the community. His own home, from which he had been taken, was just terrible. It wasn't even his parents' fault, just fate, money problems and sickness. . . .

"Jimmy had just been taken off hyperactivity drugs. Basically he was withdrawn, very uneasy and nervous, often shaking and crying at his desk. But there were also his unpredictable outbursts of defiance. One of them happened during a whole-group reading lesson, when Jimmy suddenly declared loudly, 'This book stinks.' There was instant silence, and I could feel every other child in the class just watching me to see how I'd react.

"I ought to make it clear that I've got a good situation, nothing like the mass of problems that many teachers are presented with. The kids were on my side—and they knew I was on their side— and they were horrified at first that Jimmy was fighting me. But they were watching and listening, practically holding their breaths.

"I simply said, 'OK, Jimmy. Quiet down,' and the lesson went on without further incident.

"I suppose that I could have been angry at Jimmy for messing up my neat classroom climate. But anger just didn't seem to fit the situation. Not that I don't get angry sometimes. I don't even have to say anything—the children can see it in my eyes. They know there are standards of acceptable behavior—not nice and sweet and quiet, but acceptable ways of living with themselves, so that none of them feels threatened. For example, they can always talk, but not so loud that it keeps other children from working. They usually know there are quiet times and times to cut loose. . . .

"Jimmy's case, of course, wasn't one of those fleeting problems between children which consists of grudges or punches and ends with a little crying and is then forgotten. What I did with Jimmy, I suppose, was simply to *pay attention*. I didn't shower him with affection when he was crying and withdrawn. I didn't shower him with anger when he acted the way he did during reading. I did let him know that I was paying attention to how he felt.

"The change in Jimmy was just amazing. After a few months, he was able to stop going to the clinic. One day I assigned simple-sentence writing to the class and Jimmy wrote, 'Our teacher is happy,' and when I saw it I added, 'because Jimmy is in my class.'

AN ECONOMY OF ATTENTION

Paying attention emerges as a key phrase which would be so easy to pick up if it weren't so easy to put down. Yes, children's demands for attention are constant and diverse and, in a class of 20 or more, seemingly insatiable. But the teacher here is talking about an economy of attention which allocates the teacher's scarce time with some efficiency among a number of different and demanding personalities. The teacher recognizes and acknowledges the child's feelings in a few words:

"You're unhappy."

"You're angry."

"You're having trouble with this problem, aren't you?"

"You're full of mischief today."

"You're noisy."

"You're restless."

Serious time-and-motion studies might indeed be made to compare the process of paying attention to the process which in one sweep notes disruptive behavior, proclaims or publicizes it to the class and punishes it. Psychologists and experienced teachers observe that troubled children, lacking simpler forms of attention, will settle for sarcasm, humiliating scoldings or even physical punishment. (This has often been interpreted, somohow, to mean that children *want* punishment—a conclusion which would seem absurd on its face except in a few truly pathological cases. Harsh physical or verbal punishment, as a debatable issue, may be entirely outside the scope of a book on resolving classroom conflict. Very wise and successful teachers—and a number of defeated ex-teachers —have provided whole catalogues of reasons why the *actual* use of harsh punishment doesn't work: It destroys the order it is supposed to preserve; it develops huge hostilities, subdued or overt, which may destroy the child one way or the other; it escalates, breeding counterattacks and increasing violence. And it is inhumane.) Supposing that children with problems will not settle for being ignored, it would benefit the teacher to perfect the thriftiest forms of paying attention.

IDENTIFY THE BEHAVIOR

A difficult and necessary preliminary to thrifty "attention paying" requires the identification of those behaviors which warrant attention and those which do not. To do this, one must draw the line between children's behavior that is "natural," transient and of little long-range consequence, and behavior that truly threatens children and the harmony of their classroom society. What behavior can be ignored, tolerated or accommodated? What behavior cannot be borne or absorbed?

An elementary school principal stewed about teachers' inability or unwillingness to make such discriminations:

"We over-react. We take a push or a shove or a shout and make a Supreme Court case out of it. Most of these 'big' problems ought to be kept about two inches off the ground. Instead we often end up with a major judge-and-jury scene about what happened—or what was *about* to happen—and most of the officials weren't even there to collect evidence. Sometimes we have to remember that school is a children's world, and that children skip, sing, whistle, yell, run, fight and cry, and most of their problems among themselves

29

Kids should know there are standards of acceptable behavior—not just sweet and quiet, but acceptable ways of living with themselves.

would be momentary if we'd let them be. Sending them to the principal is overkill. Sending them home to the parents is really the end of the line. I've had parents get information about a simple learning problem and say to me, 'Why didn't you tell us about this earlier? We would have beaten him up for you.' And then I have parents like the man I was talking to, socially, the other night, who announced, 'I've taught my kid never to throw the first punch but always throw the last one.' I asked the man if he ran his business that way.''

Conflict behavior, in individual children and among children, arises, if it is going to, in what the social scientists call the *interface*

between the child and the teacher/school concept of how things ought to be. A tour led by the principal quoted above, for example, included one classroom in which a fourth grade boy sprawled over his desk, sound asleep. Such a spectacle might be deemed a disruptive problem—or might, in fact, have been one—in many classrooms (as would an unusual hair style, unusual clothing or an unusually prominent student handicap, such as stuttering). Here it was not. The boy, recently re-evaluated and moved up from a class for the retarded, still tended to work in the morning at a peak which left him completely exhausted by noon. The other children in the class seemed to understand, and went on with their own afternoon

31

work as though nothing unusual was happening. And nothing was.

Given the opportunity or the inclination, hundreds of teachers may find hundreds of ways to assure that interface is workable. One respondent teacher who did this with particular flair developed a technique he calls "engineering conflict." He argues that open conflict in a strong classroom framework is preferable to underlying conflict which is persistently corroding:

"I think that nagging behavior problems have to be put into some kind of classroom arena where they can be clarified. Students ought to be able to examine the consequences of their behavior in a dramatic and relevant way. If I have to, I set it up that way.

"Let me give some reasons for this idea out of my own experience as a student. In grade school and into high school, I was a verbal troublemaker. Smart, but arrogant as hell. I made it a habit to be supercritical of other students' work, laying on the sarcasm when they made mistakes and tearing them apart when they did something like giving a sloppy oral report. Once one of my teachers called me aside and told me to be nicer to other students or my grades would suffer. Now that really didn't make much difference in the way I behaved. Much later on, I finally realized that the real consequence of the way I acted was making enemies for no good reason out of people who could have been my friends. My teacher should have talked to me about that, instead of threatening me—I knew it was a weak threat—with poor marks. The personal consequences remain long after the grades—which we teachers tend to think of as important rewards—are forgotten.

"That's why I'd rather see conflict out front instead of lurking underground. For example, if I had a chronic bully, I wouldn't seat him away from everyone else. I'd put him between the weakest kid in the class and the strongest kid in the class, with full expectation there would be some action. If the bully picked on the weak one, he would be picked on by the strong one. You can argue that I would be setting up the weak child and making a 'policeman' out of the strong one, but doing this would create a contained situation we could talk about in terms of actual consequences related to a system of values. In turn, this could bring on self-made changes in a student's behavior—the only way that behavior is really going to change is voluntarily.

"In the same way, I'd thrust a withdrawn kid into a situation where his participation was absolutely vital. Now, team sports or committee work don't fill the bill here; in either case, the child can hang back and be ignored. A familiar structure which works is the tangram exercise in which several students are given an envelope

32

containing five cardboard segments, and each student is supposed
to form a square out of the segments without talking or taking any
segments from another student. Yet no one child has all the segments needed, and no one can make a square unless there is un-
spoken sharing.[3] A similar exercise involves a short detective story
cut into parts which are distributed to four or five students. The
mystery won't be solved unless every student provides the "clues"
he's holding. Both of these exercises cause genuine frustration and
pressure for all students concerned. The withdrawn student can
come to a self-realization that his participation is needed, or take
some heavy outer stress that tells him the same thing. In either case,
there are immediate consequences that can be examined, in a way
that school punishments and rewards cannot."

GIVE THEM THE CHANCE TO CHANGE
Suspending judgment, the teacher may find serious conflict re-
solvable in the framework of a classroom society:

"Two of my third grade boys got into a fight—a real donnybrook,
bad enough to get all the other children out of their seats and into a
'ringside' audience. I dragged them apart, and I was ready to ship
them out instantly. But it seemed important to do something with
all the concerned spectators standing by. What was the problem?
The cause turned out to be commendable. One boy had taken a book
from the classroom library that the second boy had already started
and wanted to finish —it was an 'I had it first' situation.

"How was that going to be resolved? Some of the little judges
were busily assigning blame and punishments. The first boy should
have put the book in his own basket instead of leaving it in the
library. Oh, but he was halfway through it and deserved the right
to finish. . . . Someone finally suggested that the two boys should
be sentenced to read the book together. That worked. Much more
happily than I would have expected."

As one teacher observed, "Few kids are really freaked out, but
most of them are normally neurotic." There are times when almost
any student may need to be told clearly by the teacher that his/her
behavior is out of place, and then to be offered not derision or
punishment, but a chance at active alternative behavior. A kindergarten teacher puts it as simply as this:

"Some little children don't seem to grasp the idea that hitting

---

David Weitzman, "Break the Ice with Five Squares," Learning Magazine, vol. 3,
no. 1 (Aug./Sept. 1974), pp. 32–37.

hurts other people. When one of them hits another, I do tell him that. And I say I don't like it. And I ask him if he wouldn't mind punching a pillow or waiting until recess to go outside and kick the fence. Once in a while I'm taken seriously, which is all right. Usually, the situation turns to amusement, which is better yet."

A child who doesn't feel threatened and is offered a decent opportunity to switch his behavior may be encouraged to focus on his own disruptive behavior:

"Tony, what are you doing?"

"Tearing paper, that's all."

"I think you're keeping some of the other children from paying attention to their project. And isn't that sort of an unnecessary mess?'

"Yeah."

"How about picking up the scraps. And then you can be a big help to me by putting these books back on the library shelf."

The names of this game are understanding, communication patience and civility. The game may have to be extra long with some children who are particularly troubled. But even then it is likely to consume less time, temper and mutual dignity than the other game of judge, yell and punish.

The conflict problems of children in the classroom might be summarized in:

CONCEPTS AND GENERALIZATIONS

1. As a wise jurist reminded us, "No generalization is wholly true, not even this one."[4]

2. At first meeting, the child's problems and potential for conflict behavior are not the teacher's fault. After that, the teacher is a least half responsible for the quality of the relationship.

3. Before thinking about techniques, teachers might reflect on their own primal notions: Do you consider all children inherently good, all children inherently evil or some children inherently good and others inherently evil? Do you believe in the good vs. evil concept at all?

4. Though school rules of conduct may seem to be absolute and indivisible, they are imposed in many different ways by many

---

[4]Commonly attributed to Supreme Court Justice Oliver Wendell Holmes, Jr., and cited in *The Great Quotations*, compiled by George Seldes, New York: Pocket Books, 1967, p. 409.

different teachers. Rules and routines may be completely dominant in some classrooms, completely recessive in others. Conflict behavior may be put aside, and seeming "success" achieved, in either the total-discipline or total-learning classroom. But most teachers are faced with a mixed bag.

5. Referral of a child's problems to specialists is an ethical cop-out if the teacher knows the specialists haven't the time or resources to resolve the problem.

6. All factors considered, the classroom teacher may be the most effective psychological therapist available. Psychologists themselves say as much.

7. A teacher who stays calm and restrains judgment or punishment can use the following tools of conflict resolution:

a. Pay attention to children's behavior, acknowledging their feelings with the greatest possible economy of phrase—don't smother them with anger, don't smother them with love.

b. If a child's behavior bothers you and/or the class, say so. Identify the behavior clearly and say clearly why it is disturbing you. Don't be permissive; that is, don't leave unmentioned those behaviors that you or anybody else in the class can't stand.

c. Consider the constructive uses of conflict in the classroom. The appearance of conflict *can* be obliterated by a combination of tough authority and time-filling routine, but conflict behaviors —hostility, fear, cynicism, arrogance, the urge to lie or steal and others—may only be temporarily suppressed by children who will express them elsewhere and later on. Conflict behavior, brought into the open in a mature classroom society, may offer effective lessons which ultimately reward children far more than the short-range benefits of school grades and deportment credits.

CHAPTER 3

CHILD VS. TEACHER VS. CHILD VS. TEACHER.....

Ablack third grade boy disrupts the classroom with repeated insolence, gradually tinged with profanity, that he aims at his young white male teacher. Where's the resolution? Psychologist Ron McMullen suggests one way:

"Suppose that the teacher is ready to blow that kid right out of the classroom. And suppose that the kid doesn't care; he feels tough, and he *knows* the teacher thinks he's an impossible little sonofabitch. Also suppose that, because I'm an outsider, they'd both trust me.

"So I'd lie to both of them:

"To the boy, 'Man, you've really got that teacher frustrated. He thinks you've got a lot of smarts. But he can't get to you because you're too busy leaning on him. He's mad because he thinks he can really help you make it, and you aren't letting him.'

"And to the teacher, 'That kid's scared to death of you. All that bravado is just a fear reaction. He's really terrified, and he's striking out in panic with all the weapons he's got. All he needs to know is that you're not trying to kill him.'

"Each one of them comes into contact with a new percept that can be used in their relationship, and there is a strong possibility that it can work out in these terms."

The "lies," of course, may not be lies at all, but actually impressions which are available, though unused, in the thoughts (or fantasies) of the boy *and* the teacher. It is practical to imagine (as noted earlier in another comment by McMullen) that the teacher himself might function effectively in the psychologist's role. Assuming that the boy has been conditioned for combat on deadly emotional battlegrounds in the family and community (so there is nothing essentially "personal" in his attacks on the teacher), a therapeutic effort by the teacher would be indicated.

What appears to be an attack by the child on the teacher, however, may indeed be a two-way aggression. The teacher is cloaked in a role which defines itself as loving learning and all children equally, and knowing what is best for the child's welfare. This role is to be honored (the military analogy dictates that, "You salute the uniform, not the officer") and never rightfully attacked. Yet there is always a person wearing the cloak as a disguise. Personal hangups —an ever-so-mild racism or elitism or fussiness—may be submerged not too deeply inside the teacher's role. Such aberrations need not be flagrant to cause conflict; as both scholarly and pop psychology books have told us over and over again in recent years, the causes of conflict may not reside largely in either party but rather "in the relationship."

CONFLICT BEHAVIOR MAY BE MULTIPLIED
BY THE SYSTEM . . .

The implications in terms of classroom discipline and conflict can be rather startling:

"It is in this area [the bilateral aspects of classroom conflict] that the greatest potential for misunderstandings exists, simply because we habitually place the discipline problem in students, not in the relationships between students and teachers, which is where it belongs. If that is true—and we are convinced it is—then the relationships must be changed if the discipline problem is to be solved. Furthermore (and this realization still sends chills down our spines), if the system of schooling places teachers and students in untenable relationships, but only the students are punished, then it is patently unjust."[1]

As imposing as that statement is, it may yet be too narrowly rational. For, beyond the personal natures and experiences of student and teacher, and beyond the testable structure of the system, run primitive currents of myth, folklore, prejudice and prattle which perhaps qualify the educational culture for greater attention from the anthropologist. The conflict potential of both child and teacher may be multiplied not only by the system but by separate kinds of mumbo-jumbo.

Sophisticated efforts to develop a professional "image" for teachers, and the really vast gains over a century in the competence and urbanity of teachers, have left untouched an underground flow of folk attitudes which describe teachers on a range from hobgoblinish to grotesquely comic. The characterizations of teachers by early-school-age children to pre-school siblings and playmates include spectacular atrocity stories which have often been transmitted over the years, just like children's jingles and jump-rope rhymes. In playing "school," the little "teacher" is often remarkably officious and punitive in a style not learned in school (not *always*, anyway) but rather absorbed as part of persisting play culture.

Myths may persist and grow even among children in the real world of school. "I know for certain that there are four or five children from my classes in the past few years who have sworn to other children that I paddled them," reported one teacher. "It happens even though I abhor punishment and have never touched a child in anger from the day I started teaching."

---

[1] Alfred Alschuler and John V. Shea, "The Discipline Game: Playing Without Losers," *Learning* Magazine (August/September 1974), p. 84.

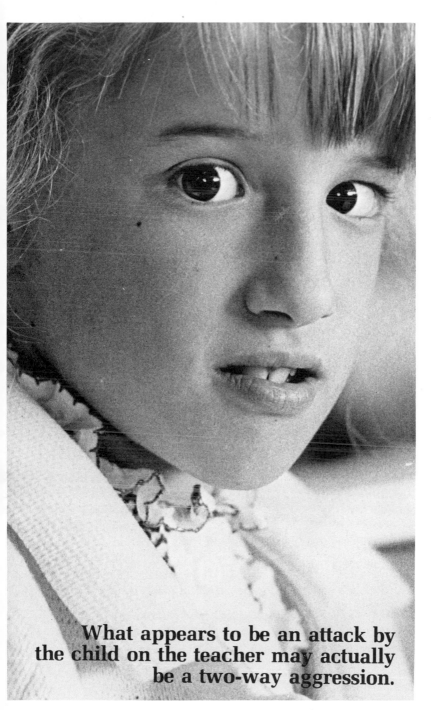

What appears to be an attack by
the child on the teacher may actually
be a two-way aggression.

... BY THE CHILD ...

The society of students, from first grade through high school and perhaps beyond that, has a remarkable propensity for developing fantasies about the private lives and personalities of teachers. An especially juicy inventiveness about faculty sex may begin to flourish as early as fourth or fifth grade.

No extensive scientific study (as far as the author knows) has ever been made of the teacher-myth as a cultural phenomenon. But many of us, if we think back, participated in it, wondering what the teacher was like as a person and then filling the void of information with wild misconstructions. Teachers remark on some fragments of their evidence:

☐ "Some of the children in my class seem absolutely flabbergasted to meet me by chance outside the classroom, in the supermarket or the park. They literally gape at me, and seem to be thinking, 'Is it really true that the *teacher* shops for groceries, too, or takes walks just like other people?' "

☐ "Though I was teaching regularly in a city junior high school, I had time available to work two days a week in a neighborhood nursery school. I was surprised at first that these very young children all called me 'Teacher'—'Help me, Teacher' or 'Look at this, Teacher.' I was a little annoyed because I equated this form of address with 'Hi, Teach,' which my urban teen-agers used regularly as a provocative kind of joke or insult. I complained to the regular nursery school teacher that I'd much rather be called by my name than by my title. She said not to be concerned about it, that the children weren't at all hostile, but they already had a clear understanding of the role being more important than the person in it. I was surprised, anyway, to find that a person is going to be identified by role—even by 3-year-old children—unless he really asserts his personality."

All of this might be dismissed as primitive or childish.[2] Yet the evidence suggests that the teacher is less known as a person than as part of a detrimental stereotype among children *and* their parents. And the stereotype, as we all know, makes a far easier target for conflict behavior than a known, living individual.

---

[2]Childlike wonderings and gossipy fantasizing about teachers' lives probably persist unmatured among adults in many parts of small-town America. Teachers of course, aren't the only professional group subject to this sort of thing. Nurses physicians, lawyers, athletes and airline stewardesses suffer the same treatment But the teacher-myths are the most widely accessible, the earliest developed and the longest held.

... BY PARENTS ...

Why parents share in this stereotyping is difficult to explain. They may simply be expressing their childhood feelings in modulated form. Permissive parents especially may see the teacher *in loco parentis* as the Mr. Hyde half of the Jekyll-Hyde duality. It happens like this:

"I was reading at about 11:30 at night when the phone rang. Believe it or not, it was the mother of one of my fourth graders, telling me that Johnny wouldn't go to bed and would I please *tell* him to go to bed. 'Put him on,' I said. When he came to the phone, I just quietly said, 'Go to bed,' and hung up. A few minutes later, the mother called back gratefully and said it had worked like a charm. . . . What's the world coming to?"

Or this:

"I was downtown and I ran into this businessman I know. He was with his little daughter and he introduced us: 'Mary, this is Miss _____. Now you're going to have to watch out for her when you go to school next year because she's going to make you behave —or else.' I was furious, and I scolded him then and there for giving the child such a terrible impression. I suppose that just confirmed for her what he'd just told her."

If the teachers who contributed to this study represent a fair sampling of the situation, the parent-teacher relationship is in a terrible state of disrepair and disrepute. A middle school principal suggested that "problems can be solved 99 times out of 100 if teachers would call parents and ask for help—face-to-face—and not through form letters." But one teacher summed up her feelings quite differently:

"I never ask a parent to work in class. It never works. It creates a problem for the parent and for that parent's child in the class. I never ask parents to help at home with a child's learning weakness, either. It's tiring for both the child and the parent and they're too close to each other; it simply creates new tensions and conflict. And I don't enjoy having parents come to school. They feel uncomfortable and nervous, and they seem to feel they have to protect their child from me. It's impossible to keep discussion at a general, impersonal level."

Another teacher suggested a palliative guideline: "When I must confer with parents, I call them and talk to them like another parent —which I am, after all. I dispense with jargon and all the other signs of teaching authority, and do the best I can to relate their parental problems to my parental problems. It helps."

Despite the reservations of many teachers, the most widely endorsed form of building parent relationships—and preventing conflict—is the recruitment of parent helpers for the classroom.[3] Though the risks are evident, classroom participation looks like the most favorable way of having the parent see the child in context, and converse with the teacher at working level in active, relevant terms.

. . . AND BY THE TEACHER

Up to this point, discussion has concentrated on those conflict-causing superstitions and misperceptions which afflict teachers on a culture-wide scale. But teachers themselves participate, with various shades of willingness and many conscientious misgivings, in underground communications of their own. The official super-structure is the student permanent file, which has become scan-dalous in its very scope. Developed originally as a useful reference to the "whole child," the permanent file has now been criticized as constituting "a serious threat to individual privacy in the United States" because of the misuse of its masses of intimate information both by unauthorized school personnel and by representatives of non-school agencies.[4]

Most of the materials in the permanent file—such as standardized test scores, health records and forms summarizing achievement and behavior—are official and systemic (that is, the teacher must maintain "I was only following orders" unless prepared to go head-on against broad administrative policies). The teacher's anecdotal comments on student behavior, which are collected for filing by most school systems, involve a much wider range of teacher discretion—and possible complicity and culpability—in situations like these:

". . . A father attending a routine parent-teacher conference about his outgoing son could discover in the boy's anecdotal record comments that he was 'strangely introspective' in the third grade, 'unnaturally interested in girls' in the fifth and had developed 'peculiar political ideas' by the time he was 12. . . ."

"A teacher of a child entering a new school gets this summary of the student's past academic year: 'A real sickie—absent, truant,

---

[3]Chapters 4 and 5 will cover this option at greater length.

[4]The comments are derived and the excerpts are taken from "Cumulative Records: Assault on Privacy" by Diane Divoky, *Learning* Magazine (September 1973), pp. 18–23.

44

The teacher is less known as a person than as part of a detrimental stereotype.

stubborn and very dull. Is verbal only about outside, irrelevant facts. Can barely read (which was huge accomplishment to get this far). Have fun.' "

The nature of such value judgments lies totally within the control and responsibility of any teacher who makes them. Since the contribution is nominally confidential and unmonitored, some teachers may exercise a passionate flair for spilling out their deepest anxieties and hostilities in regard to certain children. Such a personal catharsis can be accomplished without regard for long-range accuracy or long-range consequences. Yet the statements are in writing. Where the records become accessible by law to parents, or to students themselves, there is the chance of accountability to standards of precision or fairness.

THE GRAPEVINE: A WEAPON OF WAR

No such restraints loom over the grapevine in many teachers' lounges, which often functions as an iniquitous supplement to the students' permanent records. Discussion of students' lives and school performances is a strangely preoccupying activity during thousands of teacher coffee breaks. The conversation (unless it is somehow tape-recorded in current fashion) is not attributable; it tends to gain force as it loses warrantability and identification with its source. Anyone who has ever observed the worst of such sessions can label them for what they are: not shoptalk or professional feedback but plain gossip. At its most vehement, the talk in the teachers' lounge flows in parallel streams to the children's fable-making about teachers; and it can create monsters just as fearsome.

Curiously, classroom teachers seem to be the group which refers to students' permanent records less frequently than any other body of school or government officialdom.[5] Why? It might reflect a general lack of time or diligence, but it might as well suggest teachers' concern for bias prevention. Many teachers are torn between what they see as their responsibility to examine the files and their responsibility to ignore any poison therein:

"I'd like to judge kids for myself. Maybe there are medical disabilities or certain learning disabilities that I should know about right at the start of the year. And I'd hope that other teachers would have been constructive and professional in their comments. But I'd rather wait a while, to make up my own mind."

Another teacher has made up his mind:

---

[5]Ibid., p. 19.

"I just don't look at student records. And, as far as I know, my colleagues, if they examine the files at all, wait at least until November or December."

It appears in sampling, then, that teachers feel the need to read student files with blinders on. But it's more difficult for them to wear ear plugs.

A graduate school teacher, with past experience at every school level, complains about the prevalence of tale-telling:

"Even here, where the students may have had years of teaching experience themselves, we have a student underground and a faculty underground carrying information that is usually colorful and sometimes irresponsible. You will hear talk about a student you've never met. And then one semester you'll find her in your class and say to yourself, 'Well, here she is.' Like it or not, you have preconceptions. Especially in smaller schools, this sort of thing affects not just individuals but whole classes. The whole class acquires a reputation for being quiet or unruly or obnoxious or dull. And you prepare yourself for it in those terms."

The metaphors of "defense" and "war" apply rather aptly here, as do the warnings of sages over the centuries that the war prepared for will likely be fought. In terms of classroom conflict, the teacher who anticipates disruption from particular students or a class, and who sets up elaborate techniques to forestall problems, is not unlikely to find the defenses themselves instigating conflict.

Flaws in the school grapevine often make it untrustworthy. A previous teacher's judgment may have been inaccurate for a number of reasons, or right only at the time it was made. Children change rapidly, in any case, by themselves. One teacher comments:

"During the summer, I sometimes find myself thinking, 'God, I hope I don't get that kid.' And then I find I've got that one, and that one, and that one. But I try to stay loose, and keep looking for some good in all of them. They sense that, and they respond pretty well."

PROMISES AREN'T ENOUGH

All of this argues for what Herbert Kohl calls the teacher's "state of suspended expectations."[6] Teachers may keep in mind that they must work to have students suspend expectations as well. Disciplinarians frequently point out that students trust and respect a teacher who establishes rules and punishments, and then applies the code thoroughly and even-handedly. But students don't tend to

---

[6]Herbert R. Kohl, The Open Classroom (New York: Random House, 1969), p. 20.

We had
the beginnings
of trust.

expect that. Nor do they expect better promises to be fulfilled:

"I taught eighth graders one year in a private school which gave teachers great latitude. So, at the start of the year, I told the class they would all be marked A throughout the year, regardless of performance or behavior or even attendance in class. They didn't believe me. They *knew* school wasn't that way. They *knew* that teachers are not to be trusted. When I did give all of them A's at the end of the first quarter, some of them began to believe I might have meant what I said. But they weren't sure. When I gave everyone A's at mid-year, most of them finally believed me. We had the beginnings of trust. The point is if you're going to do anything different you have to do what you say you'll do. Promises aren't enough— they want proof."

Trust is a highly personalized matter, extremely fragile under those forces—differing environments, differing perceptions, differing roles in the system and exaggeratedly different cultural roles—which keep students and teachers apart.

CONFLICTS OFTEN START WITH SMALL PROBLEMS— BUT GROW TO GIANT PROPORTIONS

There are clues, nevertheless, that the problems of classroom conflict in the suburbs and inner city schools may be closer to being one than convention would suggest. In either locale, the escalation seems often to start with talking, or getting out of lines, or failing to complete homework. A young inner-city teacher describes this fourth grade incident:

"On Wednesday I just got disgusted with [Roger's] behavior. He had been disrupting the class all morning. He had not had his [failing] test papers signed. He had not done his homework and he kept getting out of his seat and raising his hands in front of the other boys.

"In the afternoon, after I saw that he had been [getting out of line] in the yard again, I had him stand in the back of the room and hold his books. He didn't say anything. He went to the back of the room and smiled. He had a ridiculous grin on his face as if to say, 'Make me stand in the back of the room. What do I care? I don't care who you are or what you are.' Yet his eyes seemed to be brimming with tears and I wasn't quite sure exactly how he felt.

"Well, he was standing in the back of the room with his books and I was trying to conduct a lesson but every few minutes I would hear a crash—Roger had dropped his books. I said, 'Pick them up and don't make a sound!'

"He dropped them again and laughed. He thought it was very

funny—it was good exercise bending down to pick up books.

"Finally, after dropping them three or four times, I thought the whole thing was ridiculous. There was no need for him to drop them. I left the lesson and went to the back of the room. I took him by the shoulders and started to reprimand him: 'Who do you think you are? This is not funny! There is certainly nothing to laugh at! If you don't know how to behave, it isn't funny. It's a sad situation!'

"Then filth came out of Roger's mouth and he was raving mad. 'Get the _____ off me!' His arms were swinging, not particularly at me but just to get away from me.

" 'That's enough from you!' I said, and I took him down to the principal's office. . . ."[7]

This indeed is only the beginning of a rapidly intensifying process—involving parent and principal meetings and new confrontations with the child—which aggravates as it deteriorates. The plain question is whether or not it is worth all the agony it involves.

THEY NEED TO HAVE CHOICES

The practical alternatives to all this may seem so dramatically platitudinous, so excessively simple, as to defy belief. Suppose that classroom conflicts could be kept to the very level at which they happen. Suppose that teacher and child could shuck off the whole weight of institutional and cultural roles and confront each other as people, even though they may be people with admittedly different needs. And suppose that the child, and the teacher, can consider choices of acceptable behavior which may be available.

The instant response in many cases will be this: "I *will not negotiate* with a *child*." The mandate may be supplemented with a list of clearly non-negotiable behaviors: running in front of trucks, hitting with sticks or stones or pointed objects, vandalism, arson, assault and battery, grand theft, taking dope. . . . So be it. Yet the absolute refusal to bargain may turn a child's reluctance to eat his peas or stand quietly in line or write his paragraph, into a vast battle of elemental forces. The child and the teacher in this case may be mere symbols of an eternal conflict between ruler and ruled.

Is the offering of choices impractical, unnatural, or humiliating to either party? Many teachers say no, including this one:

"I've convinced myself that children—even as young as they are

---

[7]Estelle Fuchs, *Teachers Talk: Views from Inside City Schools* (Garden City, N.Y.: Doubleday Anchor Original, 1969), pp. 46–47.

in my ungraded primary—never do anything unless it's voluntary. In effect, you let them have their own way or you'll get nothing out of them. No, I don't mean permissiveness; they don't really *want* to do things all that awful. You just let them have a choice, usually. The children do daybooks, for example, and I just ask them for one picture and one word, and usually get a good deal more. But sometimes less. One young fellow came into my classroom with an awful chip on his shoulder—I think it was put there by his parents, who considered themselves experts on open education. The boy actually hid his daybook to keep from looking at his work. Then he told me he wasn't doing any work; he didn't like writing and he would not do it. So I asked him to write down what he did want to do. It wasn't meant to be a trick, by the way, and he sensed that. He wrote, 'Play with clay. Make a mess with paint.' I proposed that he do half of what he wanted to do and half of what I wanted him to do. That seemed fair to him. Fortunately, he chose the clay half of his little list, and I got a picture a day in his daybook for a time until he started writing quite a lot."

Another primary teacher offers her classes a highly sophisticated educational concept:

"I tell the children that I don't teach anybody else. I taught myself, and I can tell them how I did that so they can teach themselves. But they have to find their own ways, too.

"Of course, this can't be done when just one way is mandated in math or reading, and we have to worry about children catching up or getting to grade level. They have to have choices. If conventional reading materials don't work, they should be able to work with their own language, their anger, their anything. If a child is hung up on the regular math materials, we need to let him handle coins or objects and build out from there."

STRONG-ARM TACTICS MAKE MATTERS WORSE
Choices may play an important part in behavior, too, as this teacher confirms:

"If there's no constant threat of punishment, kids don't have to cheat and lie. Suppose that this boy is throwing rocks out in the playground, a real no-no, but at least he hasn't hurt anybody yet. What you don't do is land on him and send him to the principal or send him home. And you don't ever ask him *why*. He'll probably fake you out with 27 different reasons, including the weather and his deprived infancy. You simply ask him what he has been doing. And he says, 'Throwing rocks.' And you ask him for his own value judgment: 'Is throwing rocks the best thing you can do?' And he says, 'No.' And you ask him what else he could be doing. And he says, 'Playing kickball.' So you ask him to check back with you for a few days to let you know how the kickball is going. About 99 out of a 100 kids respond to this approach, knowing they did something wrong and grateful you let them off the hook—once.

"Think of the same situation as it might apply to an adult. You make a mistake at work and the boss lays you out in front of 10 other people. How would you feel? Or what if he just said quietly, 'You goofed. Now what can we do to fix it?' You'd feel better, and probably work better.''

Even where punishment persists, some teachers begin a choice process there:

"When my sixth graders are truant or skip assignments or mess up in other ways, I give them an option of staying after school or working up something in their free time. I read somewhere about a school where kids could choose to get paddled and get it over with. But I'm not ready for that one.''

CLARIFY BEHAVIOR WITHOUT MAKING JUDGMENTS

Ideas like these have a good percentage of psychological fiber, and relate to organized processes which are called *client-centered therapy* (Carl Rogers), *reality therapy* (William Glasser), *acceptant responses* (Richard Curwin and Barbara Fuhrmann), or *active listening* (Thomas Gordon). In principle, all of these terms cover ways of clarifying behavior without making judgments about it. This process gives another person the opportunity to examine his own behavior and to do something about it, independently and responsibly.

One teacher recalls a tragicomic situation where a veteran teacher did not follow a behavior-clarifying process:

"Probably the most unpleasant incident in my teaching career— so far—happened when one of my fifth grade boys defied one of my colleagues in the cafeteria. The boy was nervous with something of a reputation for being a classroom problem, but I was surprised that he'd be so insolent—calling her an 'old lady' or an 'old bag'— I'm not exactly certain because she didn't care to repeat it. It happened because she was on cafeteria duty and he wouldn't eat his vegetables. He finished his hamburger and wanted seconds. But he hadn't eaten his vegetables. My colleague reminded him, correctly, that school rules said he had to finish everything on his plate before he could have seconds. He argued that his parents had told him he didn't have to eat the vegetables. She insisted, and one thing led to another, and the boy ended up in trouble.

I proposed that he do half of
what he wanted to do and half of
what I wanted him to do.

"I was really caught in the middle. The other teacher wanted disciplinary action because of the insult to her and especially to her long years of experience. And she claimed it would be for my good as well as hers. I decided to take the matter to the parents rather than the principal. That was probably a mistake, because both of them came in terribly upset and defensive. As it ended up, we had several meetings without much in the way of results, just angrily skirting around the issue until it wore itself out. One day, while all this was going on, the boy volunteered to me the idea that my colleague 'ought to be retired.' I was silently tempted to agree. On the other hand, I couldn't see where all of this was doing the boy or his parents or me or the school much good."

If the veteran teacher in the case had followed an organized process, she might have said to the student:

"You're upset. Your parents have told you that you don't have to eat your vegetables. But the school rules say that you have to finish your first helping, including your vegetables, before you can have seconds. So what should we do about that?"

The teacher would not have made the authoritarian response (which she did), which goes something like this: "You want to have seconds without cleaning your plate. This makes you unruly. In fact, you should eat your vegetables, anyway. You are unruly *and* wasteful."

Nor would the teacher have made the permissive response, which goes something like this: "Poor child. I understand, because I've never liked vegetables, either. Why don't you just dump those when nobody's looking and then get some of that hamburger you enjoy so much?"

The first response simply recognizes the problem, and leaves room for resolution of the conflict, preferably by the student himself. *Both* the other responses, authoritarian-negative-hard or permissive-positive-soft, impose judgments which establish control but also make a person-person relationship more difficult.

The conflict problems of teachers and children in the classroom might be summarized in:

INFERENCES AND HYPOTHESES

1. Teachers and students trying to resolve their conflicts as people may need to peel away thick layers of role-playing and folklore which feed conflict.

2. The folklore image of the teacher is stern and sour, and may

persist in the minds of some people (parents, for instance) well past childhood. The teacher who asserts personhood may avoid attacks aimed at the stereotype.

3. The official school files and the unofficial faculty/staff grapevine create preconceptions which in turn may breed conflict. The advance word on students may be inaccurate or outdated. Effective teachers seem to make up their own minds about students, with minimum feasible reference to file cards or scuttlebutt.

4. Teachers seem to regard parental help as a lost cause in conflict situations. But potential teacher-parent conflicts may be eased in two ways:

a. Let the parent know you are more than a teacher, being also gardener, driver, shopper, hobbyist, sports fan, parent, voter, or otherwise representative of broad human interests.

b. Encourage parents to work in your classroom, so they, too, may be called teacher and think of themselves that way.

5. Remember that students may not trust you, and will not expect you to change just because you say you will change. In making threats or promises, it is well to remember that students may not believe you.

6. If any conflict is perceived as one between proper authority and unprivileged childhood, the tiniest incident may incite major friction.

7. Conflict between teacher and child should be accommodated as much as possible at the person-person level.

8. Classroom conflict may be resolved or prevented by the teacher offering the child choices of behavior or learning approaches. This may be accomplished without demeaning either party.

9. Conflict behavior may be resolved by talking about it with the student in a non-judgmental way (imposing neither authoritarian nor permissive decisions) and letting the student make his own value decisions and choices of optional behavior.

CHAPTER 4

CHILD VS. SYSTEM VS. CHILD VS. SYSTEM.....

IT IS fine and sensitive to talk about person-to-person relationships resolving classroom conflict or dissolving the causes of it. That can happen, as the past two chapters suggest, when teacher and student are able to meet at the very point of a conflict and try alternative new behaviors. This demands that *both* cast off the weight of their own environmental disabilities, of cultural roles conveyed by folklore or gossip and of those rule-responses which can only be described as extensions of self.[1]

What remains, and cannot be easily abandoned by personal will, is what we know so ominously as "The System." Teachers have been praised and blamed for running their classrooms as little independent kingdoms. The System pulls all those kingdoms together into a multi-billion-dollar enterprise, structured to suit the expectations of parents and the larger community. Seen as a

---

[1]Rules are often what we make of them. The teacher may have a personal proclivity to emphasize or exaggerate selected rules about neatness or quiet or clean language, while giving only routine attention to most others. Reciprocating, the child may selectively resist certain rules and routines—like standing in line or writing every day or cleaning one's plate—while accepting most others.

context of classroom disruption, The System presents three major kinds of ambivalence:

1. The benefits of education are widely endorsed. But The System presses these benefits upon clients who may be unwilling to receive them. Children must go to school. Just as they tell their parents, "I didn't ask to be born," they may tell their teachers, "I don't want to be here." Both arguments are crudely true and uncontradictable.

2. Though it aspires to develop self-control and self-discipline in children, The System must function around tight and easily communicated norms for behavior and academic progress. But these norms are necessarily much too simple to cover the great range of children's day-to-day human responses.

3. Though it may seem to be constantly embattled, The System in fact is remarkably effective in disarming potential attacks and gaining general compliance with school goals. On the other hand, The System is extremely vulnerable to passive resistance. At the classroom level, passive conflict may be a problem much more bitter and frustrating than active disruption.

SWALLOW IT WHOLE, IGNORE IT—OR TRANSLATE IT

The contradictions are vast, and the teacher's life—satisfaction that his/her efforts really make a difference in the lives of children—

depends on recognizing the contradictions. The teacher who swallows The System whole, thus trying to embody it, dines on double-edged razor blades. The teacher can assume that all children should be grateful for the opportunity of schooling, that all mandated lessons and codes of behavior are to be followed to the letter, that letter-grade reporting to parents is effective because it is simple and commonly understood and that obedience equals self-discipline. But that teacher is virtually doomed to a heavy succession of conflicts. Believing that The System is coherent and deserves total allegiance, that teacher is betrayed, left with a plaintive "Why?" as hopes for the children's growth and the teacher's own self-confidence erode under a steady drip of little altercations and little insults.

An equally dismal but quicker fate may be in store for those zealous young teachers who wish that The System would go away and leave them alone with the children. Their minds and intentions are pure; they diligently consume a whole catalogue of open, humanistic techniques. But they cannot bear to be interrupted by The System. Yet, they soon find, The System is persistent and enduring and, in one form or another, essential. What hurts them so much is not conflict with administration, parents, or community; that's to be expected, even if its intensity is far greater than foreseen. As it turns out, however, the children themselves are distrustful of sudden freedom. They seem to prefer a known tyranny to the unknowns of free choice and personal responsibility. So, with hostility and conflict emerging where least expected, the idealist teacher often deserts or grows cynical.

Many teachers in the middle range between these two types have conflict resolution skills suited for something more than mere survival. They neither glorify The System nor try to bring it crashing down. Instead they serve as mediators, translators, guides and brokers between the children and The System. They try to moderate The System when it is necessary and possible; they give fair warning when The System cannot or will not be changed.

RECOGNIZE REALITY

The matter of mandatory school attendance is a prime test of the teacher's acknowledgment of reality. There are valid debates, of course, about whether school attendance should be compulsory or not. To argue the matter as a true-false question, however, is to be purposefully unconscious. Children must come to school; the law says so. The comparison between some schools and some prisons, furthermore, is almost old hat even among not-so-radical educators. The points of similarity—bells, marching in line, passes, the physical separation of people, the constant vigilance of the staff, the pretense of "rehabilitating" the inmates, etc.—are irresistible to the metaphor-makers who have worn this one almost into the ground. Very young students will keep on saying that they are "serving their time" or "going back to jail"—and some will really mean it. Sometimes this feeling can only be acknowledged, even by a teacher who would like to do more:

"Some students in a city junior high school are more difficult than others, but most of them are fun to be with. One I remember just got to the point where I couldn't do any more for him. He was almost 16 and still in the seventh grade. I couldn't tell him that he had any social or economic reason for being there. His friends were out working already. He had a job with relatives waiting for him as soon as his birthday came. Some days he'd come to class, then walk out, then come back, then leave again. I didn't have any rewards or punishments that could mean anything to him. The other students seemed to understand that this boy's situation was special. They didn't let it bother them much. The boy went his own way. I couldn't dislike him for that."

At this level, the recognition of reality can keep a potential cause of disruption from actually being disruptive. The same insight may be relevant to conflict resolution at a much earlier level, as this kindergarten teacher suggests:

"When a child causes an upset early in the year, I have to feel that it's his problem, too. After all, he's been wrenched away from a comfortable home, and maybe a Mommy who loved him, and the Lord only knows how much preparation he really should have to make him accept that. I'm sick of people who seem to think that not wanting to come to school is a kind of sickness. I don't slobber over the child, but I let him know in my own way that he may have a right to feel indignant about it. And I try to let him know that wanting to come to school is a gradual thing. That depends on me."

BEING CONSISTENT IS OFTEN HARD WORK

This willingness to come to school is perhaps the very first step toward self-control and self-discipline. These are qualities about which school people demonstrate considerable semantic confusion when objectives are proposed and documented:

"One of the most challenging and often one of the most baffling problems parents and teachers have to face is that of channeling the ceaseless activities of children into an organized pattern of self-controlled behavior. . . .

61

Passive conflict may be a
problem much more bitter
and frustrating than active disruption.

"Domination probably plays a part in growth: if self-control breaks down, the responsible adult must be ready to control the situation. Certainly obedience is a part: a child who cannot obey cannot learn to control himself. Also self-direction, with the aid of expert guidance, is essential to growth."[2]

The same document includes suggestions for teachers:

"Cooperative making of rules as the need arises may gain the interest of children while teacher-imposed rules may create resistance. . . .

"Well-established routine minimizes behavior problems. . . .

"Expecting one type of behavior today and another tomorrow leads only to confusion and discouragement. Be consistent."[3]

Yes, be consistent. The trouble with advice from The System is that it often takes a firm, uncompromising stand on *both* horns of the classroom teacher's dilemma. Much of the advice cited above may be classified as *oxymoron*, a literary figure of speech which combines opposite or contradictory terms, i.e., *loud silence, happy sorrow, bright darkness*, or, as in the selection, *organized self-control, obedient self-control, guided self-direction* and, perhaps, *cooperative making of rules/well-established routine*. More elaborately, we may say, "You will democratically elect any student representative of your choice, though we of course have the right to reject your candidate," or, more simply, "You may read any book you choose. Please bring it to me for approval first." The literature and school declarations of objectives may include a number of nobly standing individual statements which combine as inconsistencies, evident even to a child. The classroom teacher, meanwhile, will probably have to smother conflict with an authoritarian "No" or resolve it with a surrendering "Yes," as in this case:

"Jimmy was a troubled child who felt that no one else in my first grade liked him very much. Besides, he wanted to wear his jacket all the time. Well, I tried to reason with him, telling him that he'd be too warm in class and that he might catch cold when he went out on the playground. He was very firm about it, though, and I finally let him do it. Well, he wore that jacket indoors and

---

[2]Frances Holliday, "A Positive Approach to Elementary School Discipline," *Discipline in the Classroom* (Washington, D.C.: National Education Association, 1969), p. 31.

[3]Ibid., pp. 31–32.

out *all* year long. And he didn't get too warm. And he didn't catch cold. But he did seem to make friends.

"Other little boys want to wear baseball caps all the time, and I had a little girl who often wanted to wear her mittens all day long. I let them do it. On the other hand, I don't permit gum chewing. Well, I shouldn't say that I would never, never permit it. So far, I've just suggested to my gum chewers that they shouldn't do it unless every other child has a piece of gum, too. That seems to seem reasonable to them, so my classroom hasn't ever been all gummed up. I suppose that's what you'd call drawing the line, but I don't really know where the line should be."

RULES SHOULD BE BROAD PRINCIPLES, NOT INCENTIVE FOR AN EVASION GAME

In another school situation, gum chewing came to the legitimized side of the line:

"Remember the days when a kid caught chewing gum had it stuck on his nose for the day and had to write, 'I will not chew gum' a few thousand times? We never tried to humiliate a kid that way —all you get back for that is resentment—but we did spend a lot of time hassling about gum. Then, finally, we started to wonder why we should burn ourselves out over that kind of unenforceable law. So now the kids chew gum when they want to, as long as they don't chomp like cows. That's not a rule, either, by the way. Actually, we've got only three rules left:

1. Whatever you start, you have the responsibility to finish. If you can't finish it, you are responsible for getting help (your buddy, teachers, friends).
2. Try to put things back where they belong. This is our school. We are responsible for keeping it neat and clean.
3. Try not to 'bug' anyone else who is working or playing.

"Those rules seem to cover most situations pretty well. If necessary, the kids and the teachers will add or subtract. For now, everybody seems to understand what they're about."[4]

The logic of limited rule-making may seem slipshod to some teachers and many administrators, who would read it to say that rules not made cannot be broken, therefore virtually all student behavior is defined as acceptable. Defenders of the practice can point as high as the U.S. Constitution, whose genius lies in general language that can be interpreted over time to fit the circumstances of a case and the gravity of it in a framework of change.

By contrast, many of the more lengthy and exquisitely detailed school codes seem almost made to be broken. Disciplinarians observe that rules, if they are not to be held in contempt, must be enforced thoroughly and even-handedly. Yet some school codes are so extensive that the number of unseen and/or impulsive and/or contemptuous violations multiplies. The rules themselves make possible a game in which students evade an authority with neither the time nor the omnipresence to enforce itself. Where this sort of general conflict is happening, the classroom teacher might devise an excellent exercise of editing and distilling the school code into broad principles. At the least, it may help students conceptualize what the detailed code is really intended to mean. At best, it may start a school trend toward clarity and understanding.

A CHILD'S DECIDING WHAT TO LEARN IS WIDELY CONSIDERED UNTHINKABLE

Control or self-control of social behavior is a prominent issue between the child and The System. Conflict over the content of learning is less strident. The school view of student self-discipline in learning seems limited to *how* the child carries out learning tasks assigned by the teacher and The System. Giving a child self-control over *what* he is to learn is widely taken to be an unthinkable idea: "How can a student know what he is supposed to learn when he doesn't know enough to know?"[5]

The potential for conflict over learning decisions nevertheless

---

The three rule rule comes from the Chester Elementary School in Chester, Connecticut. Learning Magazine reported on one kindergarten teacher's posting of two rules: (1) "You don't hurt anybody, on the inside or the outside." (2) "You clean up after yourself." (Catherine Healy and Henry S. Resnik, "The People's Choice for Kindergarten," Learning Magazine, [February 1974], p. 32.) Dr. Thomas Gordon reports on a junior high school in which a teacher-student group edited the student behavior code down to two rules: (1) "No one has the right to interfere with another's learning," and (2) "No one has the right physically to harm another." Thomas Gordon, Parent Effectiveness Training [New York: Wyden, 1970], pp. 301–302.)

Exception must be made here for the teachers and theorists—and perhaps the children—in the fully conceived, fully functioning open classroom. Here the children will indeed generate their own learning initiatives. But such classrooms are extremely rare. Most open classroom teachers find it essential to mandate or negotiate basic content and skills units (even if only to provide standards of comparison between children in the open classroom and traditional classrooms). Systems of individualized instruction and contract learning also promise wider choices in learning. In practically all cases, however, the *basic* decisions about what is to be learned are well outside the child's reach and often beyond the teacher's influence.

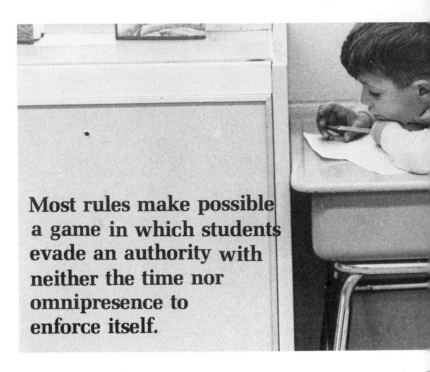

Most rules make possible a game in which students evade an authority with neither the time nor omnipresence to enforce itself.

reveals itself in observations like this one from an inner-city school psychologist asked to test a troubled fifth grader for retardation:

"Following [the] first of several testing sessions, I seek out some of Gaspard's former teachers; he has, after all, spent six years in this same school. They all consider him totally illiterate, because, although he has filled composition books with words and phrases of a high order of vocabulary, punctuation is totally lacking and his syntax is rather personal. He is considered a 'good boy,' because he is quiet in class; he could not be emotionally disturbed since he does not attack the children around him; all agree that he is 'very retarded.' The fact that his many elaborate drawings and involved compositions reveal great concentration, persistence, recall of technical details, and creative imagination—traits which any reader of popular family magazines ought to know are counter indicative of mental retardation—does not impress them; the sole criterion of mental normality accepted by these teachers is verbal fluency."[6]

---

[6]Stephen B. Goldman, "Notes of a Green School Psychologist," *Urban Review* (October 1969), vol. 4, no. 2, p. 20.

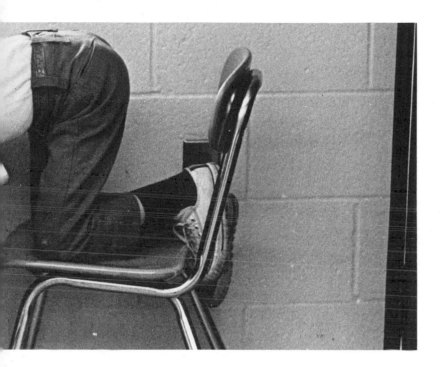

Consider the conflict faced by this seventh grade teacher:

"This boy had me licked. I understood he was a serious trouble-maker in other classes, but he'd come into my English section and sit in the back row reading his own books—anything but what we were reading in class. What got to me was that the books weren't trash; they were *good books*. In fact, they were higher level than most of what we were doing in class. I didn't challenge the boy, though I did talk to the principal about the matter. I figured I'd rather have the boy reading than causing an uproar. I guess I was afraid to try making something constructive out of his 'independent study.' The boy flunked all my tests and the course. It didn't matter to him. But I'd estimate he read 30 to 40 fine books during the year—and I really believe he wasn't faking."

"WHY ARE WE STUDYING THIS?"

Students rarely raise behavioral/intellectual conflicts with such flair. But at very early levels they start to ask the perennial question, "Why are we studying this?" That should be regarded by the teacher as a conflict question, deserving of more than stock answers.

The whole content of school instruction, after all, is a mere frag-ment of the vast universe of knowledge (which, we keep reminding ourselves, is steadily "exploding" into greater vastness). The fragment is then sub-fragmented into skills sequences and curricular levels, many of which are heavily debatable on an internal, professional level. The outsider seems quite reasonable in asking how the school knows that its program comprises the best of all knowledge for all children. The educator who stonewalls in response, insisting that The System *does* know best, risks heavy odds against him. For the serious debater can propose knowledge substitutions at a ratio of hundreds to the one the educator chooses to defend.

The student's "Why are we studying this?", set against the full scope of the issue, should seem like a good and not impertinent question. The teacher who would resolve the conflict implied in the question needs honest responses about the fact that school knowledge is selective, and that—whether didactic, inquiry-oriented, or value-oriented—it can be made a basis for learning how to learn. If that justification can't truly be made or is not enough for the clients, the teacher should allow the possibility that children can act as fair critics. A change in presentation may be indicated, or, where possible, a broad change in content. The open-minded teacher, guided by open-minded students, knows best what these changes have to be.

The wonder of The System, down to classroom level, is its seeming immunity from really destructive questions. Americans support school goals in much the same way they support that other great institution, the personal income tax. The comparison is not facetious. Both systems ask for compliant participation and usually get it, without great coercion, from people in astonishing millions. Schooling and taxpaying are considered to be vitally important, even though many people may not like them very much.

The income tax system is satisfied with eventual conformity, despite taxpayers' strongly expressed feelings of inequity and confusion as well as their traditional pattern of gleeful minor cheating in the process. The educational system cannot thrive as well on the bare compliance of parents and students. Yet there is a prevailing sense of school as something important to be done, something important to be gotten over with, rather than something to be vitally experienced.

Some students prod The System with sharp instruments to see if it is as important as it is reputed to be—or if it will explode instead. They present obvious conflict problems. Far greater numbers of children come grimly to school to do their learning chores to the satisfaction of their parents and relatives, their teachers and

68

prospective teachers, their employers of some years hence and almost anyone but themselves. Among them are the conflict problems which surround the teacher, not like a storm but like a dulling haze: apathy, inaccessibility, impersonality, sullenness, blithe disregard of classroom processes, disguised or open boredom, mechanical responsiveness, obsequiousness. Probably the teacher's greatest frustration is the sense of not "getting through" to these young people as an instructor or a person. Some of these children seem so uncaring that a sensitive teacher may finally even try to provoke them into open conflict; better a hostile emotion than none at all.

Perhaps this is a new breed of children, basically modified by lightning changes in the society, or perhaps the above are ageless characteristics of childhood. Teachers, at any rate, are perplexed:
□ "One day after school I stopped and listened in on a group of sixth graders standing just outside the door. There were about six of them and they seemed to be having a lively conversation. I was dumbfounded. None of them was talking about the same thing at all. No one connected to the others. It was just an acting job for each one of them. But no one had an audience. They weren't even listening to each other. The question is how I'm ever going to expect them to listen attentively to me when they don't even listen to their friends outside the classroom. They're really insecure. I usually concentrate on the subject in class, but I think I've got to bring this problem—about how they treat each other—into the classroom for my own sake."
□ "I've tried to schedule class sessions for discussion, but it has just been awfully uncomfortable. These kids, only fourth graders, are so absolutely *bland*. Maybe they've seen so much and heard so much on TV that they can't get excited about any of the little questions here. Anyway, I will not plan any more discussions until it really matters, and then we're going to have our meeting on the spot. What it will take will be an incident dramatic enough to make them think. I don't know what it will be, and I'm not looking forward to it, necessarily—or maybe I am."
□ "I can't get over the peaks and valleys in what these kids know. Our middle school used to be the high school, so it has a fairly good lab. One boy, very smart bookwise, was doing a demonstration which involved an egg. I suggested that he might save himself a mess by hard-boiling it. So he took the egg and put it right on the ring stand over the Bunsen burner; he was going to 'boil' it right over the open flame! You wonder how he could have lived in a family for 12 years without knowing what boiling an egg means."

SCHOOL: A PLACE WHERE PARENTS KNOW BEST?

The System seems to involve parents and other people in the community in seeing education as a fixed formula for progress: Follow the numbers to success. One teacher comments:

"Are children over-compliant? Heavens, yes. You can really see the sins of the father being visited upon the children. We have many parents who—as they recall it now, anyway—worked very hard at school tasks they hated and played by rules they disliked. And now they've made it. So they see a magical connection between one thing and the other, and want their children to repeat the experience exactly. They keep insisting that their children 'have to know the basic facts.' What they mean by that in math, for instance, is that the children should be given the kind of time tests the parents remember from 25 years ago: a whole set of repetitive arithmetic examples given to see how well and how fast the child could answer. Today, instead, we might give 6-year-olds their addition and subtraction facts and then ask them to make combinations of their own with cards numbered 1 through 9. The children work alone and together and find ways of teaching themselves. It's open but it's highly structured, too. I have to work hard to convince parents that this is basic facts plus something extra in terms of thinking and motivation. Discussions like this aren't a bad thing, of course. They get parents thinking about important issues rather than petty things."

Roland Barth's chronicle of an open-classroom experiment in a deprived inner-city neighborhood dismisses the thought that formula thinking is only a middle-class characteristic. He quotes one of the protesting black parents:

"We want our children to go to high school, to college, to get a good, white-collar job, to have a home, a car, and raise a family. In short, we want them to do what *you* (whites) have done.

"You have had a certain kind of educational experience. . . . If our children have the same kind of educational experience, *they too* will make it.

"But, since our children are starting with many strikes against them, since many are already behind in reading, writing, and arithmetic, and self-control, they will have to have your educational experience, only *more so*. More respect, more obedience, more authority, more homework, more books, more discipline."[7]

---

[7]Roland S. Barth, *Open Education and the American School* (New York: Agathon Press, 1972), p. 156.

"Why am I studying this?"

CHILDREN ARE BRAINWASHED INTO FOLLOWING THE PARENTAL FORMULA

When the children themselves seem to find it expedient or important to endorse the parental formula, the classroom teacher may be thoroughly dismayed:

☐ "The parents love math because they think it's so cut and dried. I send the children home with two pages of homework problems and the parents are happy. But I'm afraid I've got a whole bunch of kids who know that 2 + 2 = 4, but don't even care why. In science, of course, what looks like 2 + 2 can be almost 3 or almost 5, depending on conditions and measuring devices, which are never exactly the same. The kids want answers quickly. If I ask them to measure the boiling point of water, they can't understand why they should do that. The textbook says water boils at 212 degrees. I point out that the textbook leaves out a lot of important conditions. But they're frustrated and impatient when they have to sit down and make the measurements. All they want is a 'fact' to take home and spout at Mom and Dad and Uncle Harry."

☐ "My eighth graders were involved in a unit on colonialism and cultural contacts, studying the meeting of English colonists and American Indians. I thought they would be very interested in Indian sign language, which is part of my little grab-bag of skills. I started to run through some sign-language sentences. Most of the class seemed interested, but one boy started to get restless and finally raised his hand.

'Are we going to have a test on this?' he asked.

'Of course not,' I said, thinking I was reassuring him.

'Then why are you taking time for it?'

"That was the most terrible putdown! Honestly, I just wanted to give up all ideas of helping them think, and give them textbook and tests for the rest of the year. They're brainwashed from the cradle with that whole idea of getting grades so they can be successful."

Barth describes behavioral conflicts in the inner city school:

". . . One teacher asked a child, 'Robert, why can't you behave yourself?' He replied that he didn't know how to. 'What do you want me to do to you?' the teacher asked. 'Hit me,' he said. . . . In another instance, the instructional coordinator told a fourth-grade math class he was working with that the teacher in the adjoining class was complaining about the noise level. 'How are we going to keep the noise down?' he asked. Their responses were revealing:

Tape our mouths shut.

Kick the noisy ones out of class.

Punish us.

Let's go somewhere else for math.
Send a note home to the bad people's parents. . . .[8]

To infer from these various experiences that children *want* drill and *want* punishment may be shortsighted or self-serving. Teachers beset by classroom conflict, active and/or passive, ought to find a way, whatever the assumed risks, of bringing themselves, children and parents together and asking them openly if pain, humiliation and onerous, boring work are truly "good for you." As individuals, and as perpetrators or recipients, most of us find such processes painful. But this first step should not be the last.

In further discussions of the sort, the conflict-resolving teacher might keep in mind this summary:

UNDERSTANDINGS, VOWS AND DISAVOWALS

1. Don't pretend to children that The System is clear and straightforward. Do your best to protect them from its ambiguities, or at least to admit its contradictions.

2. Remember that the littlest child is pushed to school by law, and may have reason to object. Also remember that his willingness to come, regardless of the law, is a first step in self-control.

3. Reflect on the mutually exclusive differences between disciplining one's self and being disciplined by others. (The two may necessarily exist in alternating sequences—but they will never blend.)

4. Occasionally review the code of behavior and ask, "Is this rule necessary —or does it foment the conflict it is allegedly designed to prevent?"

5. Never pretend that school knowledge or teacher knowledge is the best or most essential of all the world has to offer.

6. Never be forced into a position where you must tell children that what they're doing now will only be important later and elsewhere. Work with yourself and children and parents to find ways of making school count here and now.

7. Recognize the bored compliance of children and parents as a conflict problem at least equal in severity to disruptive rebellion. Remind children and especially parents that drudging obedience in insufferable tasks is the very opposite of productive, self-disciplined freedom.

---

[8]Ibid., pp. 139–140.

CHAPTER 5

CHILD/ TEACHER VS. SYSTEM VS. CHILD/ TEACHER VS. SYSTEM.....

THE teacher as moderator gracefully interjects his/her person and experience between the child and The System, understanding the inconsistencies on each side and trying to help both sides tolerate their basic incompatibilities. If that role description sounds hyperbolic, think for a moment of a teacher trying to explain to a child why he *must* read when, at the moment and for his foreseeable future, he doesn't *want* to. That is conflict, and the teacher's challenge in trying to resolve it is awesome. Yet it is by no means the effective teacher's greatest trial. For a time may come—will come—when the teacher is irresistibly pressed to take sides, joining either the children or The System almost without compromise in a conflict issue. The possibilities in such a case might be represented in three classes of dialogue:

    1. Child: Why do we have to study *this*?
       Teacher: You seem to be very unhappy with it.
       Child: Yeah, it's dumb stuff.
       Teacher: Some people think it's fun, and some think it's

important for you to know when you grow up and work. You don't think so?

Child: Well, maybe. . . .

The importance of certain school rules and school work, including even reading, are not self-evident to every child (or, for that matter, to many sensitive adult observers of education). The teacher as moderator withholds prescriptions and tries to help the child come to his own terms, responsibly and voluntarily, with activities that are deemed generally important.

2. Child: Why do we have to study *this*?

Teacher: (impatiently) Because we must. Now let's have a little more respect from you.

Here the teacher as front-person for The System has *the* answer to virtually any piecemeal conflict situation—even though the conflict may soon be transposed to other, more varied settings. But the teacher needn't be a devoted authoritarian to want to be where the power is: sometimes the power response is dictated by mere economy of time and temper. It's the frequency of this response that matters. It may get to be an awful habit. But sometimes the teacher finds the power words unspeakable, as in:

3. Child: Why do we have to study this?
   Teacher: God only knows.

An implausible dialogue, perhaps, but not unthinkable. Few reasoning teachers are thoroughly committed to everything they are supposed to do. Sometimes they want to protest openly. Knowing they are regarded as The System's good soldiers, however, they try mightily to keep from breaking ranks, as in this parent-teacher debate:

"My son's vocabulary assignments are awful. They don't seem to have anything to do with useful language, or meanings, or shades of meaning, or anything but passing a quiz the next day."

"I must admit I don't like to teach vocabulary this way. But the public insists on it."

"The public?"

"The children have been testing poorly on vocabulary for the past couple of years. There's some alarm about that."

"But the exercises I've seen seem to be filled with misleading definitions, or partial definitions, or meaningless definitions. It's hard to see how they'll help a kid to love words, or even to pass any outside testing. You're the professional. Can't you use some other exercises, anyway?"

"Well. . . ."

"It seems not."

"I'll have to have you talk to our language arts committee."

If the one parent is right, then the public (other parents? supervisors? administrators?) must be wrong. At any rate the teacher is fated to sound courteously vague and incompetent. The conflict question is fragmentary; it can only be dealt with in the grossest terms by committees, associations, or the union—when they get to it. For the time, it will be added to all the rest of the small conflicts which hang unfinished in mid-air, in the community and in the classroom.

SMALL ISSUES MAY TAKE ON SERIOUS PROPORTIONS UNDER SCHOOL STANDARDS

Problems which are ostensibly very simple and minor often take on grave form in the school milieu:

"The snow fence which guarded a slope at the end of the playground had somehow been knocked down one night. It was an unhappy problem for the primary children—for me too—because their playground ball kept rolling over the fence, down the slope and

78

into the road, and of course I had to go get it each time. I sent several requests to the office for the repair of the fence and the two broken posts. Nothing happened. Then one afternoon the ball rolled down the slope again and a man driving by calmly stopped his car, got out, took the ball and drove away! The children couldn't believe what had happened. They were hurt and upset. So I had them draw pictures and write what they could about the incident in their own ways. The work was impressive because the children were so troubled about what happened. I packed all the material into a big envelope and sent it to the principal. That got quick action, without another word of discussion. I was relieved it didn't go any further than that."

Relief might be the appropriate feeling, since there are situations (fortunately in the extreme) where teachers are fired for pushing small issues and particularly for assuming that children may have a right to complaint and petition. It should hardly be a wonder that children's issues often seem childish:

"We have a Student Council in the middle school, but they seem to spend all their time on picayune matters, like wanting the right to chew gum or to twirl their yo-yos in the corridors between classes (we're departmentalized). When it comes to major activities they seem to fall apart for lack of organization and effort."

A symbolic democracy may have to stand or fall on small tests, nevertheless, demanding somewhat risky cooperation (not supervision) from involved adults. Another Student Council situation seemed to survive the test:

"My second graders just had this innocent inability to understand why snowball throwing was absolutely banned. We talked about all the strong reasons for the rule, but they still seemed to insist on the pure joy of it, swearing that they would never want to throw snowballs at each other. All there was to do, finally, was send a letter to the Student Council. I was surprised when the older students approved what amounted to a snowball target range in the playground. It seems to work so far. I wouldn't make predictions about how long that will last, but it may. And it is fun."

TOTAL ACCEPTANCE OF THE SYSTEM LESSENS FREEDOM AND SELF-COMPETENCE

Seemingly minor matters take on great weight when they reflect systemic issues among teachers themselves. Here are two incidents from schools where "closed" classrooms and open classrooms tried to co-exist:

☐ "I was substituting in a third grade classroom which was ob-

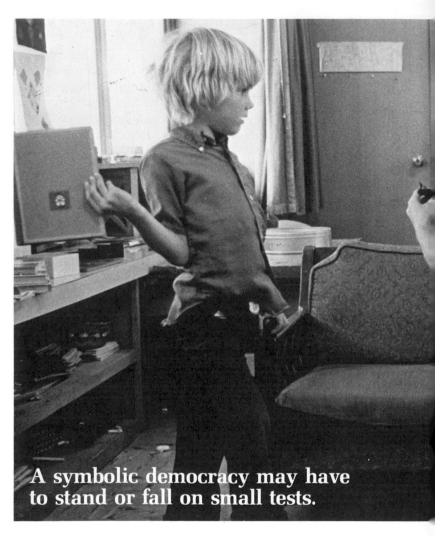

A symbolic democracy may have to stand or fall on small tests.

viously well-organized by the regular teacher. None of the usual substitute high jinks happened; the children were well-behaved and very businesslike. Late in the morning, though, there was something that really mystified me. There was a knock on the door and I asked one of the boys in the class to answer it. It was a little girl, who handed him a paper. He closed the door and then almost vehemently tore the paper into bits and threw them into the wastebasket. What's this all about? The paper, I found, was the little newspaper published by the open classroom children. And the children in the third grade classroom had standing orders to destroy it on

sight, without ever reading it. Now, isn't that an indecent thing to do to children?"

☐ "I run a contained fifth grade classroom that is managed firmly, but I don't think it's rigid. For example, the kids are planning a history exercise where we'll relive a typical day of Colonial schoolchildren, walking a few miles after they get off the school bus, cooking lunch outside, doing chores, using slates all day and so on. We also have classroom meetings every Wednesday where the kids can set their own rules of behavior and sound off about school subjects, too. They're a little restless right now because an open classroom has moved in next door and those kids can go in and out of the classroom whenever they want to, and seem to be allowed to slam the door as hard as they want to. We talk a lot about it, and I try to keep my kids as well-informed as I can about everything that's going on in the school. It's gotten us into some interesting discussions about what the open classroom is supposed to do, and how. What it comes down to is a decision to wait and see how the other class makes out. We figure they need time to get on their own track."

The two cases suggest striking differences in the ways children and teachers learn to treat each other as people, resolving conflict or escalating it to the point where it can only be managed by imposed uniformity—in other words, by The System. The delegation of conflict problems in this way clearly lessens the teacher's freedom of action and must put some teachers on the down side of the self-competence scale. At a particular level of disagreement with The System, teachers seem to perceive just one kind of response:

"When you're told to teach from just one book, or told you may never read a particular story, it's time to leave."

"When you have an administration that starts to treat you like one of the kids, you've got to go."

"If your bitterness with parents and the whole System starts to show through in the way you treat children in the classroom, you have to start thinking about getting out."

"When you begin to feel like a martyr, you'd better leave."

"If you're going to have control, you have to earn the kids' trust. If you haven't got that, you might as well go."

The content of such maxims is perhaps not half so interesting as their illustration of teachers' tendencies to draw a hypothetical line beyond which they'll call it quits. The tension is evident and perhaps timeless, though it yearns for some better resolution.

BE HONEST IN DISCLOSING YOUR ATTITUDES
A related problem lies, somewhat short of the go-line, in systemic practices that the teacher finds distasteful and barely tolerable. Should the teacher disclose these attitudes to children or not? The conflict question grows particularly strong in the area of grades and standardized testing:

□ "Tell me how to solve the nonsense about grades. As it is, I give A's to nine out of ten children, and no F's, and the children and their parents call me a tough grader. I tell them I'd just as soon give all A's, or better yet, give everyone A's when they got to that certain point of success in a project—it would just take some kids longer than others. But I haven't had any takers for that system."

☐ "The standardized reading tests were given to the first graders on the hottest day in June. What good were they to them or to me or to the school? It was certainly too late in the year for the results to help my teaching. And a whole summer's change would probably make the results useless to the next teacher. The poor children had to stew through hours of questions. It was so ridiculous. And I finally told the children so. I hope it made them feel better."

☐ "The tests sometimes are conjured up as a bag of tricks. They trick the child and all of us. For example, we use both phonic and sensory methods, where appropriate, in teaching reading to the primary children. But the tests are strongly biased toward one or the other, and some children test badly when they're actually reading at a much higher level. For another example, children are given test questions which involve a sequence of multiplications and are marked all wrong when they may only be one-fifth wrong. And the examples go on. Finally, when we realized we weren't going to do away with the testing, several other teachers and I decided we could at least dis-alarm the children about them. So we called them all together and laid it on the line—as well as we could in their language—about the imperfections of testing; and we promised the children that we wouldn't misuse the test results in judging them. No, I don't think what we said had the slightest effect on anyone's performance, unless it was to improve it."

TESTING AND DIAGNOSING—A TECHNOCRATIC NIGHTMARE TO COME?

By some local standards, of course, such tactics amount to heresy and would be treated accordingly. The burning at the stake of 10,000 teachers, however, would not change a basic paradox: The System seems to be inalterably based on enclosing children and their teacher(s) into a human relationship, and then devising more and more exotic instruments to find out from the outside what's happening inside. The technocratic dream of processing children through lines of teaching machines and testing machines doesn't seem destined to make it; yet the instruments of verification make up a bigger and bigger presence outside the classroom door. Coming atop the standardized testing movement (now old and hallowed despite the serious criticisms of it) are the accountability movement, the diagnostic movement and the learning disabilities movement. The teacher as "facilitator" would seemingly be occupied full-time in maintaining skills check lists and inventories, writing and warranting behavioral objectives and noting more and more individual differences in children. A possible precursor of more things to

The technocratic dream of
processing children through lines
of teaching and testing machines
doesn't seem destined to make it.

come within The System is offered in a *Better Homes and Gardens* article which tells parents about more than 100 forms of learning disability, estimated to afflict between 5 and 30 percent of the school population. Here are excerpts from the article:

". . . the key role in discovering children's problems and assisting with them still falls to parents. It is parents who must be aware of their children's needs and insist on help for them. . . .

"What causes learning disability? Apparently something that neither child nor parent can help. That is, learning problems seem not to stem from laziness, stupidity, lack of energy, or bad genes. Nor is it merely a matter of cultural or economic deprivation. Although the precise cause is not established, it is now assumed that a learning disability in an otherwise normal child is related to his neurological development.

"The brain cells which process information have either developed more slowly than normal, or they have been damaged, perhaps too slightly to be detected, by disease or injury. . . .

"What are the warning signs of learning disability? Once a child enters school, the signs usually become painfully apparent: The child cannot cope with fundamental work, although tests show he has the necessary potential and intelligence. The ACLD [Association for Children with Learning Disabilities] lists eight other indications, which, singly or in combination, [it] says, "should wave a red flag of warning" for parents. These are: inappropriate behavior, distractibility, apparent laziness, withdrawal, short attention span, unwillingness to cooperate, poor memory, or poor coordination. . . .

"How can learning disabilities be diagnosed? Largely by a process of elimination. If there are indications that a child is learning-disabled, the parent or teacher should get a full-scale evaluation by an interdisciplinary group of specialists in audiology, ophthalmology, neurology, pediatrics, psychology, education, language development, and child psychiatry. . . .

"It's important that parents be included in the diagnostic process, and be given a full and clear explanation of the results. While some centers do a good job of reporting results and recommendations to schools, many do not. More often, it is the parent who must carry the ball, at the very least making sure that these reports go to school personnel who make decisions about their child. . . ."[1]

---

[1]Gerald M. Knox, "What to do if your child can't learn," *Better Homes and Gardens* (September 1974), pp. 40–46. A far less credulous view of the learning disabilities movement is offered in "Education's Latest Victim: The 'LD' Kid" by Diane Divoky, *Learning* (October 1974), pp. 20–25.

CONFRONT THE SYSTEM ON YOUR OWN TERMS

Credibility is immediately strained, of course, at the thought of several million children somehow receiving the services of teams of medical specialists, when at present they are lucky to have a few minutes a year with the school psychologist or speech therapist. Yet, in a land of Manhattan and Apollo projects, all things are possible; this may be the ultimate individualization of instruction and behavioral codes. And yet, this is what some exceptional teachers have been talking about for a long time: taking a child on his own terms, taking children on their own terms, refusing to measure them by hair-thin standards of behavior or knowledge, trying to give each one time and attention, often futilely, but trying. Is there a harmony or a wide difference in The System's meaning of individualizing and the teacher's meaning of it? Teachers still close the classroom doors behind them, for better or for worse:

□ "Teachers, good ones and bad ones, perceive the classroom as independent country. They're very defensive. They know, as a rule, that no one knows how to train teachers. They know the school thinks it knows what they *ought* to be doing, but they know it's impossible for the school really to know. As a practical matter, they let no one in—another teacher, a supervisor, a principal, parents—because those people may only cause trouble."

□ "We look at a work of literature that's supposed to be valuable because the culture says so and the school says so. And the kids say, in their inimitable way, 'This reeks!' And at that point you take a look at the literature and a look at yourself. Maybe it does reek. It's a point of departure. 'So why is it so bad?' I ask them."

□ "I run an open classroom, and I believe completely in open education. But I'm not going to think of it as the gospel. Last year one mother insisted that her eight-year-old boy be enrolled in my classroom, apparently because she thought it was prestigious, the thing to do. Within a few days, she called to tell me she was really doubtful about open education and thought her Johnny should have more structure and discipline. Johnny himself seemed to be persuaded of that, looking to me for direction most of the time. Well, Momma helps pay the bills, and you can't force a child to be free any more than you can make him like routine. I set Johnny up with his own highly structured program. He was happy, worked well and perhaps had time to make up his own mind about how he finally wanted to learn."

□ "You do your own thing. You can't teach how to teach. I'm a supervisor of practice teachers, and I often see them teaching their subject brilliantly but failing to establish rapport with the kids

What's missing is old-time sensitivity. I can write behavioral objectives if I have to until they're coming out of my ears. Then I can put them aside and do my own thing. In fact, I think objectives are a good idea. But if you want to do them right, you set them up for each individual child."

Teachers like this seem to have a fierce confidence in what they're doing, even though they've known failure and may despair of ever having time enough to be thorough. They're hardly afraid of the appearance of conflict or, once it comes, of being overwhelmed by it. They confront The System as the equal of it, willing to give it professional courtesy but also insisting on their individual integrity and the children's.

When confronting The System, the conflict-resolving teacher might remember the following:

A RULE

If you've really got it as a teacher, don't close the classroom door to supervisors, parents, or anyone else. It's fair to suppose you may be infected by what they've got. On the other hand, what you've got may be catching. . . .

CHAPTER 6

FORMULAS.....

THE experience of conflict resolution, like other aspects of education, is too diverse in cause and effect to be neatly compacted. Though The System continues to insist on proliferating syllabi, curriculum outlines and procedural codes, most of us are continually more puzzled by them: the more they strive toward bare-boned simplicity, the richer they seem to become in self-contradiction, trying to serve more and more incompatible goals in fewer and fewer words.

Even the fullest and wisest description of experience is finally inadequate for the child who really must re-experience to know for himself. The same principle may apply more so in the communication of experience from teacher to teacher. The dutiful assumption that what works once in a classroom will work in another, or in the same classroom on successive days, is a step toward disappointment and possible despair. In fact, no list of classroom conflict-resolution techniques is worth a minute outside the context of the years-long reflection which made it possible. This handbook thus becomes an atlas describing the enormous range of sources of conflict. If it asks one question of the teacher, it is this: Since every conflict rises from two parties' sense of being threatened, what are you defending—the sanctity of knowledge, the dignity of adulthood, cultural or social order, the solidarity of The System, the professional image or role of the teacher, or just yourself?

If one generalization is possible from the testimony of skilled teachers, it is this: The teacher who can resolve classroom conflict has a sense of position which produces effective answers to the question above. Most often—but not always—this teacher responds: "Myself." He/she is committed to the same kind of self-direction and personal responsibility which may, in turn, be cultivated in children. The same teacher is then qualified to wonder, sensitively, if a particular child may be sick or subversive—and to seek other help.

There are well-formulated designs for conflict resolution which can work, given the commitment of teachers who aspire to self-competence (or at least to an intermission in defensive warfare). Each is deceptively simple, and accordingly easy to put down as unsophisticated. Yet it may be the simplest things—like the personal contact of a teacher and a child in a classroom—which engage the genuine subtleties of human experience and the full meaning of learning. The following references may help you toward this goal.

Schools Without Failure by William Glasser, M.D., New York, Harper & Row, 1969. Dr. William Glasser identifies the ability to give and receive love and the feeling of self-worth as the components of personal success identity. Schools, he observes, have tried to produce motivation by forceful methods: "But guns, force, threats, shame, or punishment are historically poor motivators and work (if we continue the gun example) only as long as they are pointed and as long as the person is afraid." Students must instead be involved with responsible teachers who themselves have success identities.

Reality Therapy by William Glasser, M.D., New York, Harper & Row, 1965. At the heart of Glasser's *Reality Therapy* is a focus on behavior, not emotions:

1. The child is asked (not *told*) what he is doing.
2. He is asked (not *told*) to make a value judgment about his behavior.
3. He is asked (and helped, if necessary) to select a better course of behavior.
4. He is never excused for failing to follow through on his own

commitment, nor protected from the reasonable consequences of his failing behavior; but neither is he punished. The process is repeated as many times as necessary.

Glasser's critique of the schools, beyond traditional disciplinary methods, concentrates on the "certainty principle" (the memorizing of "facts" and "right answers" as opposed to thinking), the grading system and the allied expectation that a proportion of students will fail, lack of relevance in the curriculum, irrelevant homework and lack of opportunity for democratic experience.

The positive thrust of the *Schools Without Failure* program is involved in a belief that children should have a voice in both the curriculum and the rules of their school. The vehicle is the classroom meeting where children may learn:

". . . that they have a responsibility for finding the best alternatives to a series of difficult problems, problems that they themselves help to pose. The process of stating the problem, finding reasonable alternatives, and implementing what seems to be the best alternative is education, in contrast to the present process of blindly obeying (or breaking) rules and unthinkingly echoing back right (or wrong) answers to questions raised by others. . . ."

Glasser proposes three types of classroom meetings which deal with social problem solving and student behavior, open-ended discussion of subjects intellectually or emotionally important to the children and educational diagnosis related to understanding of the school curriculum. Though the principle may seem simplistic, Glasser observes, considerable meeting practice is needed to overcome both student and teacher discomfort—a sign of how difficult conflict-resolving communication in the classroom may actually be.

Parent Effectiveness Training by Dr. Thomas Gordon, New York, Peter H. Wyden, 1971, and *Teacher Effectiveness Training* by Dr. Thomas Gordon, New York, Peter H. Wyden, 1975. The teacher in loco parentis and as a negotiator and counselor with parents may study Dr. Thomas Gordon's theories from several rich perspectives. Gordon analyzes Method I behavior (authoritarian), Method II behavior (permissive), and proposes a "no-lose" Method III of problem solving and conflict resolution. One fundamental of this system is determination—not so easy as it may seem—of who "owns" the problem, an important first step in knowing when conflicts are genuine or slowly manufactured. A central technique is *active listening*, in which adults "open the door" to a child's talk and "keep the door open," so that the child has time to think the problem out and—as may be likely—come to his own reasonable decision. Adults, Gordon points out, more often use a battery of judgmental techniques to block the child's conversation and thought. The obvious adult put-downs include judging, criticizing, blaming, ridiculing and shaming. But Gordon points out that children are put down as well by the adult's interpreting, diagnosing, psychoanalyzing, teaching and instructing. In relation to well-defined conflicts, Gordon analyzes a long list of "coping mechanisms"—responses to the use of power—which may be revealing even to experienced teachers who suppose they've seen everything.

Gordon may fairly be taken as less pragmatic than Glasser in regard to classroom realities. His techniques suggest even greater latitude for the child's responsibility and decision making, even less structure in the matter of rule making and the transmission of values which adults may consider absolute. His ideas might also be studied for a sense of how far the "limits" might logically be stretched.

Human Development Program by Dr. Harold Bessell and Dr. Uvaldo Palomares, San Diego, Human Development Training Institute, 1972. The work of Dr. Uvaldo Palomares, Dr. Harold Bessell and their colleagues—the "Magic Circle" program—represents one of the most fully implemented classroom approaches to questions of personal responsibility and interpersonal relationships. Topics for the 20-minute circle sessions have been developed through eight levels—pre-school through grade 6—and potentially for use, if the teacher chooses, every classroom day of the year. On this scale, of course, the elements of conflict behavior are constantly being examined, clarified and contained in children's discussions of how they think and feel. Topic sequences swing between the personal development areas of awareness, mastery (self-confidence) and social interaction. The simplicity/complexity of "Magic Circle" topics may be evident in a one-week social interaction segment at primary level:

Monday: Somebody Did Something That I Did Not Like
Tuesday: I Did Something That Somebody Did Not Like
Wednesday: The Teacher Did Something That I Did Not Like
Thursday: I Did Something That The Teacher Did Not Like
Friday: We Each Did Something The Other Did Not Like

To say that this sequence is unsophisticated might indeed be protesting too much; the simple questions touch on almost global conflict patterns.

The "Magic Circle" teacher is encouraged to exert leadership

It may be the simplest things—
like personal contact between teacher
and child—which engage the
full meaning of learning.

94

at the start with acceptant responses and good listening skills, but to surrender leadership and responsibility to the children as quickly as possible.

ADDITIONAL RESOURCES

The briefest study suggests that current relationships between teachers and parents are devastatingly conflict ridden. When the emotional, cultural and political costs and implications of this situation are considered, almost any positive conflict-resolving action would seem to have merit. One starting point for the teacher might be an inquiry to: Center for the Study of Parent Involvement, 502 Oakland Ave., Oakland, California 94610. Other resources in this area are "Two Generations of Volunteers: Parents," by Christopher T. Cory, and "Two Generations of Volunteers: Grandparents," by Heidi Seney, Learning, October 1974, pp. 76–83.

As the "Magic Circle" people, among others, suggest, most good conflict-resolution formulas incorporate "what master teachers do every day to instill responsibility and self-confidence in children." What these teachers have that the rest of us need, perhaps, is freedom from perceived threats, or a sense that everyone—children, parents, taxpayers, even school administrators—feels threatened each in his own way. If conflict resolution is basically the process of freeing us from these fears, there may be no better starting point than the classroom.